JEWELLERY MAKING

Jewellery Making

A Manual of Techniques

David Rider

The Crowood Press

First published in 1991 by
The Crowood Press Ltd
Ramsbury, Marlborough
Wiltshire SN8 2HR

Paperback edition 1994

British Library Cataloguing-in-Publication Data

A catalogue record for this book is available from the British Library.

ISBN 1 85223 813 5

Acknowledgements
Photographs of workshop equipment courtesy of H. S.
Walsh & Sons Ltd.
Demonstration photographs courtesy of Graham Light of
Abbey Studios
Line-drawings by David Joffe.
The drawings appearing on pages 39, 40, 152 and 153 are
reproduced with kind permission from the Assay Offices of
Great Britain.

Typeset by Inforum Typesetting, Portsmouth
Printed in Great Britain by Butler & Tanner Ltd, Frome

Contents

	Dedication	7
	Introduction	9
1	The Workshop	11
2	Hand Tools	19
3	Metals	36
4	Soldering	41
5	Polishing	49
6	Making a Ring	58
7	Findings	67
8	Surface Decoration	110
9	Projects	114
	Appendices	148
	Glossary	154
	Useful Addresses	156
	Index	158

TO ALL DYSLEXICS

Dyslexia can be overcome and lived with; it forms the negative side of the abilities balance, but can be worked to your advantage, so you should never despair.

Introduction

Jewellery in its loosest sense is one of the oldest crafts known to man, going right back in history to when natural dyes were first used to decorate and embellish the body. Tattooing is a very old form of body decoration, certainly dating back to the sixth century BC in Japan. Later, shells, feathers and bones were added to provide more sophisticated decoration and this developed into the production of the first pieces of jewellery, worn strung around the neck, wrists and ankles. Holes were pierced through the skin, particularly the ear lobes, so that decorative articles could be threaded through. Jewellery as we know it today developed when man discovered metal. For the first time permanent pieces of decoration could be fashioned from a material that was strong and hard wearing, and it soon became a specialized craft. Metal could be hammered into shape and textured by using different shaped stones. Wire could also be rolled out, opening up endless possibilities. It could be fashioned into pins, rings and hooks as well as being twisted together and made into different designs for necklaces and brooches. By the Iron Age simple tools were being developed, enabling the jewellers' art to become even more sophisticated. By the time the Romans arrived, the jewellery craftsman was certainly as skilled as today's craftsmen, bearing in mind the tools available to him.

Until the introduction of mass produced jewellery and new inexpensive materials in the early nineteenth century, jewellery was a status symbol and was almost entirely in the hands of the ruling classes. In primitive societies it represented a visible sign of the wearer's wealth and importance, and was a convenient way for them to carry their assets around with them. During the Industrial Revolution, jewellers had a boom time as the newly formed middle-class merchants were anxious to display their new-found wealth and position.

In 1300 laws were brought in to protect traders from unscrupulous competition and the public from fraud. This was in effect the start of the present system of hallmarking and was one of the earliest forms of consumer protection.

In the Elizabethan age some of the more prosperous goldsmiths and silversmiths became the forerunners of today's modern bankers. Because they had strong boxes and vaults for the safe-keeping of their precious metals and gems, local wealthy merchants started to use them to look after their own valuables. A good example of this is Childs Bank. In 1642 Francis Child became an apprentice goldsmith. He later married his boss's daughter and inherited a prosperous goldsmithing business. However, he found looking after other people's money such a profitable sideline that he abandoned his goldsmithing business and devoted himself to banking.

It was not until the advent of mass production in the late nineteenth century that jewellery became available to everyone. Inevitably this led to a decline in hand-made jewellery, although the wealthy were still demanding high quality, individually designed jewellery. The fashion boom in the 1960s saw a sharp increase in avant-garde designers, who broke away from traditional jewellery making using precious metals and stones, to experiment with a variety of other materials. Although these materials were new and experimental, the pieces were well made, as the craftsmen had been trained in the traditional techniques. This brought individually designed hand-made jewellery within the reach of a much larger section of the community for the first time.

I have aimed this book at the beginner and hobby jeweller, covering all the basic techniques that are likely to be required. I have tried to keep the instructions simple and to the point, so that the beginner does not get bogged down in too much detail. In this way I hope I can show how exciting and rewarding the jeweller's craft can be, and enable the student to move confidently on to more intricate work.

I have purposefully left out more complicated techniques such as enamelling and engraving as I feel these should not be attempted until the basics have been mastered. Jewellery is an exciting and rewarding hobby for all those with manual dexterity and a flair for design.

1 The Workshop

The workshop for the beginner need not be an elaborate affair. The area needed for working is actually very small, being concentrated mainly around the work-bench. For anyone wishing to get the feel of jewellery making, with little initial outlay, excellent results can be achieved with minimum investment in space or money. Obviously without purchasing some of the available labour-saving equipment, there will be a large investment in time. An electric polisher will reduce polishing time considerably, but if you have polished a piece by hand the end result will be just as good and probably considerably more satisfying.

If you are lucky enough to have a small room available for your workshop – even a tiny box room would be quite adequate – so much the better. If not, a work-bench can be set up almost anywhere. Formica-covered chipboard, used for kitchen units, makes an excellent solid bench. The bench must, however, be very firmly fixed as you will be carrying out precision work that requires a very steady hand.

A clamp can be purchased that will fit to any surface combining a sawing peg, a filing peg and a steel block. Other essential equipment includes:

A mouth blowtorch that can be used from a household supply.
A borax cone and tray.
A fine watercolour brush.
Alum for pickling.
A saw frame and blades.

A pair of flat pliers.
A pair of half-round pliers.
A pair of tweezers.
Three needle files, one round, one three-square and one square.
A half-round file.
A steel ruler.

This is the very minimum amount of equipment required, and while it is sufficient to give you a taste of what is involved, for the purposes of this book I assume that you will have a reasonably well-equipped workshop, containing a wider variety of hand tools, and at least a pendant motor and polishing mop.

If you are lucky enough to have space for your own small workshop, the following points should be born in mind when planning its layout.

The work-bench is where you will spend most of your time and this should be placed near a window if possible to give you plenty of natural light. Your hand tools should be arranged around this bench – a large sheet of peg-board fixed to the wall near the work-bench will hold many of the smaller tools which are in constant use. Some of these can also hang from the cut-out made in the bench (*see* page 12).

An additional sturdy bench will be required for the rolling mill, vices and draw plates. The rolling mill is a heavy piece of equipment and the bench will need to be very firmly fixed if it is to support it – preferably bolted to the floor. The rolling mill should also be bolted on to the bench.

The space used for pickling should be close to a water supply and the pickling area should be well housed to avoid spillage or splashing.

The polishing area should be well away from work areas because of the amount of fine, pervasive dust given off, and if possible a portion of the workshop should be partitioned off for this purpose. An extractor fan will greatly reduce the amount of dust, and if the motor is boxed it helps to contain the polishing waste.

A gas supply will be needed for the torches – both bottled or mains gas are suitable. Also remember not to underestimate the number of power points required. There is no substitute for as much natural light as possible, but good overhead lighting and a powerful bench light are essential.

THE WORK-BENCH

This is the most important piece of equipment in the workshop and care should be taken in its layout and construction.

A view of the author's homemade work-bench, showing the placement of the sling and constantly used tools. The soldering area is also shown with fireproof mat, blocks and a light shield to keep the area out of direct light. This enables you to see the changes in metal colour as it is heated up. The bench is placed beneath a north-facing window to obtain maximum natural light without glare.

Ideally it should be placed in front of a north-facing window, as you may find that you get too much glare from the sun if it is placed in front of a south-facing window. It should be made from solid timber at least 5cm thick to withstand heavy hammering – a cheaper version can be made from plywood. It should be firmly fixed to the floor and should be absolutely rigid. The height of the bench should suit your own height, but as a rule the top of the bench should be 1m from the floor. An adjustable stool should be

used in conjunction with the bench to obtain the ideal working height and position. Most of your time will be spent at the work-bench so it is important that your posture is correct if you are to avoid back problems and discomfort.

A semi-circle 30cm deep and 60cm across is cut out of the centre of the work-bench at the front and discarded. Suspended under this cut-out is a sling made from leather. This will catch and hold filings and other small pieces of scrap metal. Sheepskin is an ideal material for this if you are working with precious metal, as even the finest filings will not penetrate it. Plastic is, however, a cheap substitute particularly if you are working with base metals. You must be careful not to drop hot metal into the sling when soldering as it could burn a hole in the leather. If your bench is large enough for two cut-outs, you can use one solely for precious metals as this will make recycling easier.

A bench peg is bolted to the centre of the work-bench. This can take many forms, but essentially it has two main functions: as a filing peg which has a sloping surface and should be made from hardwood, and as a sawing peg which has a 'V' cut out of it. When using a piercing saw, the metal is placed over the 'V' in the peg, allowing the saw to cut through the metal into the space. The peg can also have a steel block at the back which is used for checking that the metal has a flat surface and for flattening it out if it has not.

A rack should be fitted round the edge of this cut-out to hold all the pliers. Depending on whether you are left- or right-handed, a fitting should then be fixed on to the bench front in order to take a soldering torch.

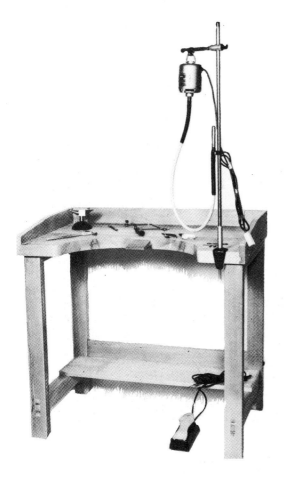

A commercially made work-bench showing how a pendant motor can be fitted.

DESIGNING

If you have room, a separate area for designing which is away from the work area would be convenient. A considerable amount of time goes into designing a piece of jewellery, so if you have a properly constructed drawing-board the work will be easier. Obviously an ordinary table is quite adequate although less comfortable. This stage of the work should never be rushed as the final appearance and balance of the piece will largely depend on the amount of care put in at this point.

SAFETY

A lot of jewellery equipment is potentially dangerous. Have a first-aid box ready. As well as the usual contents, be sure to have sterile dressings for any wounds, antiseptic liquid to wash dirty injuries, two or three cotton bandages and a crêpe bandage, bicarbonate of soda to neutralize any acid splashes and a suitable burn cream for slight burns. Remember to have a tetanus booster injection every five years.

Throughout the book I draw your attention to the various hazards as each piece of equipment is used, but the following points should be born in mind.

Acid

Acids are dangerous – always handle them with care. Keep them correctly labelled at all times and make sure they are always well corked. If acid is splashed in the eyes, rinse thoroughly in plenty of running water. If any pain persists consult your doctor. Acids should always be put in lead or heat-resistant glass bowls when in use. Bicarbonate of soda should be kept nearby to neutralize the acid, and should be thrown quickly over the affected area. Protective goggles should be worn to prevent the acid from splashing into the eyes, and a face-guard made of light plastic would be even better. Also wear an apron, because if acid splashes on to your clothes it will leave holes.

Burns

Burns can quite easily occur in a jewellery workshop if the proper precautions are not taken. Remember to keep all inflammable items away from your soldering area – even a small flame can ignite flammable liquids. Molten metal will cause a serious burn and should always be treated with great care.

Always keep long hair tied back and remember that man-made fabrics will cause a far more serious burn than natural fabrics, as they tend to leave a sticky burning residue that is difficult to remove.

Cuts

Files and saws are the most common tools involved in jewellery workshop cuts. Saw blades can break and pierce your hand. Obviously if this happens you should pull the piece out immediately. If you are unable to remove it you should go to the nearest hospital casualty department. Never use the file without its handle as the tang could easily slip and pierce your hand. If you receive a cut, apply a sterile dressing and a tight bandage to stop any bleeding. Any cut longer than 1cm should be stitched by a doctor so that it heals neatly and quickly.

Polishing Motors

Polishing motors are particularly dangerous. You *must* always tie long hair back and avoid wearing any loose clothing as these could easily become entangled in the mops or spindles causing serious injury. Open-ended pieces such as chains are particularly dangerous, as they can easily become caught in the mops, causing the spinning end to twist itself around your hand, thus severely bruising it. Always make sure the 'off' switch for any piece of machinery is within reach when you are using it.

Protective Goggles

Protective goggles should be worn when using any electric machinery to protect the eyes from fragments and dust. They should also be worn when handling acids and alkalis.

In jewellery making the most common cause of eye injury is when a metal splinter is thrown up by a piece of machinery. If this happens you should always flush the eye out immediately with plenty of water to remove any foreign body, and if this fails you should seek medical attention.

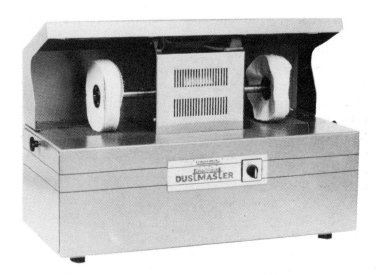

A large polishing motor with guards and an enclosed motor with a built-in dust extractor and lighting. It has easily changeable filters for scrap reclamation. This type of unit is recommended because it will cut down dust pollution, but it is rather expensive.

FIXED EQUIPMENT

Rolling Mill

This looks rather like an old-fashioned mangle and is used for rolling out metal and large-diameter square wire. The rollers are very finely polished so as not to leave any marks on the metal and for this reason careful maintenance is essential. It is important that the rollers are kept dry and clean and a thin film of oil should be applied to prevent rust. It is also important to check the bearings in the rollers and to oil them as necessary.

It is important to anneal the metal before rolling. If this is not done the metal will be stressed and could fracture. Only precious or non-ferrous metals should be used in the rolling mill, as ferrous metals such as steel will mark the rollers and could damage them beyond repair. This is a very expensive mistake, so treat the rollers with great care. Rolling mills are

A small rolling mill in use. Half the rollers are smooth for rolling sheet and the other half are grooved for rolling wire.

available that combine sheet and wire rollers, and rollers that leave a pattern on the metal are also available.

When using the rolling mill you can only accomplish the thinning process in small stages, diminishing the space gradually by careful adjustment. If you attempt to thin the metal by making too large an adjustment, it will not be rolled evenly and could become jammed. When thinning the metal it will become longer not wider as it extends in the direction in which it is being rolled.

Polishing Motor

The polishing motor is used for polishing metal to a high standard and consists of an electric motor with tapering spindles on to which a mop can be fixed. Whilst the polishing motor is comparatively safe, care must be taken and loose clothing, ties, scarves and long loose hair should either be removed or firmly secured as they can easily get caught around the spindles and mops, causing a nasty accident. When using the polisher with mops only use the lower quarter of the mop so that if the work is snatched it will be thrown away from you. Polishing is dirty work and a face-mask should be worn. If there is room, the polisher should be housed in a separate room or cubicle and an extractor fan fitted to remove the dust.

Pendant Motor

This consists of a small electric motor fixed to a flexible shaft and is operated by a foot control. The flexible shaft allows the drill to be moved very freely which gives maximum control in tricky situations. It will take very small mops and drills making it an ideal tool for intricate work.

Calico Hard

Calico Soft

Calico Stitched

Swansdown

Wool

The different types of mop that are available for use on a pendant motor.

If the pendant motor is old, care should be taken with the flexible shaft as it can wear through the outer casing. Do not bend the shaft at a sharp angle as this will cause considerable stress and wear. The pendant drill has interchangeable chucks that will hold various sizes of drill. It can

17

A pendant motor in use showing the head with a small polishing mop attached.
In the background are small blocks of polishing compound – the one on the left
is tripoli and the one on the right is rouge. Behind these is the spanner used to
loosen the chuck.

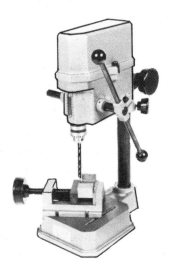

A small precision pillar drill used for drilling
vertical holes up to 6.5mm.

also hold polishing wheels, small grinding points and fraizers for texturing metal or tapering holes.

Pillar Drill

Whilst a pillar drill is not essential, most workshops have one. A clamp should be used to hold your work down when using the drill as when it breaks through the metal it can snag, causing the metal to twist round. Safety goggles should be worn to prevent swarf getting in your eyes.

18

2 Hand Tools

A jeweller's hand tools are the most important items in the workshop. They are very personalized and soon become a natural extension of his or her hands. The loss of a favourite tool becomes a major tragedy and however good the replacement, it is a long time before it becomes accepted. While a few tools can be obtained locally and are suitable for many different trades, most are specialized and can only be obtained from specialist stockists. The allied traders are to be found in the main jewellery centres and this is where you will have to purchase the large majority of your tools, although the lighter items can be purchased by mail order.

PIERCING SAW AND SAW BLADES

The piercing saw is the most important and versatile of all the tools. It is used to cut out the metal, to pierce out patterns, and to open out holes for stone setting and filing. It makes a clean, precise cut that needs very little finishing, and will cut all gauges of metal.

The saw is held vertically and cuts on the downward stroke. When inserting the blades always make sure that the teeth are facing down and out of the frame. There are two kinds of saw frames, fixed and adjustable. I suggest you use an adjustable frame as you will then be able to fit any length of saw blades.

Different gauges of metal require different blade sizes (larger sized blades have more teeth to the centimetre, and vice versa). The thicker the metal the coarser the blade, and as a guide there should be at least two teeth to the thickness of the metal. Fine blades come in sizes from 1/0 to 8/0 and coarse blades in sizes from 1 to 4. In a short while you will easily be able to choose the right blade for the metal.

The piercing saw is a 'U' shape, with a handle on one end and a short piece of metal on the other end. It has two clamping screws which hold the saw blades in place. Saw blades can be used to open out the narrowest of apertures, where a file just would not fit. In this case the blade is angled slightly so that only one face of it is cutting, thus allowing the thinnest of cuts to be enlarged.

To insert the saw blades:

1. Place the end with the short piece of metal against the bench, with the handle resting against your breastbone.
2. Take a saw blade, and with the teeth uppermost and pointing towards you (the saw cuts on the downward stroke and is held vertically when cutting), place one end of it in the handle end of the frame. When it is level tighten the screw.
3. Place the other end of the saw blade in the opposite end of the frame, but do not tighten the screw.
4. Push the handle in, and while retaining pressure on the handle, tighten the end-screw.

A piercing saw in use showing how the metal is held over the 'V' in the bench peg.
It also shows the correct way to hold the saw – note the vertical angle.

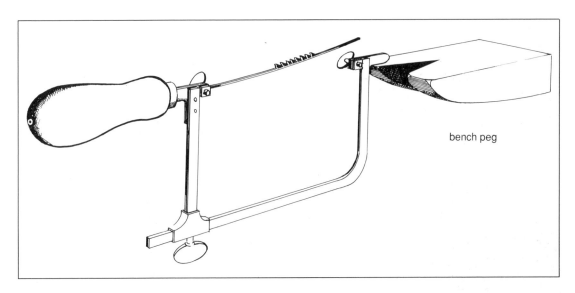

An adjustable framed piercing saw showing how the saw blade is inserted.

5.   Release the pressure on the handle. The saw blade will now be taut and should make a pinging noise when plucked.

6.   Undo this end-screw when you have finished sawing to retain the springiness in the frame.

When cutting out the work with a piercing saw, the work should be placed over the 'V' in the bench peg. To turn corners the metal must be turned while the saw is still in use or the blade will not cut a path for itself and will break.

When piercing out a design on the inside of the metal, the saw blade is inserted through a drilled hole and then the blade is tightened.

FILES

Files come in many different shapes and sizes but all have the same function: to remove surplus metal and smooth the edges. They come in various cuts from coarse to fine. The most commonly used are cut numbers 2 and 4. Cut number 2 is for general work and cut number 4 is for finishing, ready for emery paper.

Needle and Hand Files

These are the files that you will use most of the time for all general filing work, with needle files being used only where a hand file is too large. Only two or three shapes of hand file are needed, but a good selection of needle files should be kept.

Hand files come in different lengths from 7.5cm to 15cm. They are larger than needle files and will need to have a handle fixed to them. Although these files can be used without a handle with extreme caution, it is recommended that a handle is fitted, as if the file snags on some metal the tang (the metal tongue at the end of the file on which the handle fits) could rip the palm of your hand open.

21

From left to right: a small riffler file with flat ends; a larger riffler file with curved ends; two half-round files of different cuts, one of which has a handle fitted; and a flat file.

Choose a handle that you feel comfortable with and drill out a hole in the end of it with the 4mm drill to the depth of the tang. Secure the file in a vice, remembering to protect the file with soft jaws or stout cardboard. Push the handle on to the tang as far as it will go and tap on with a mallet until it is secure.

Needle files come in different lengths varying from 10cm to 18cm, the most suitable length being about 16cm. The handle is an integral part of the file.

Following is a list of file shapes, most being available as both hand and needle files:

Flat files

These are used on flat and straight surfaces and are either parallel or slightly tapered.

Half-round files

These can be used on straight edges or curved surfaces like the inside of a ring.

Three-square or triangular files

These are used for filing inside angled corners.

Square files

These are for right angles and square holes.

Round or rat-tail files

These are for round holes.

Crossing or oval files

These are for shallow curves, both sides have a different-shaped curve.

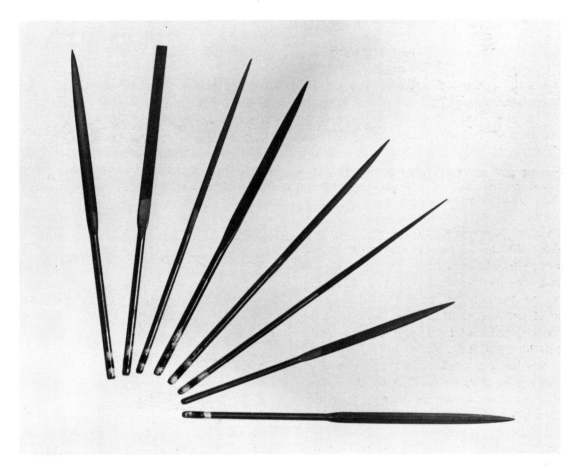

Needle files, from left to right: a half-round needle file; a flat needle file; a square needle file; a knife-edge needle file; a triangular needle file; a rat-tail needle file; crossing needle file; and a barrette file.

Barrette or safety-back files

These have one long flat filing side, the other two shallow sides being smooth. They are used where only one side of a slot is being filed and a slip could damage the other sides.

Flat files have square ends, all other files are tapered to a point.

The files most commonly used are 15cm half-round and 15cm flat hand files, and round, half-round, square, three-square and flat needle files.

Files only cut on the forward stroke, so they should not be in contact with the metal on the return stroke. It is very difficult to remove the effects of a course file so as fine a file as possible should be used, progressing all the time through finer files. The fewer the marks left by the file the easier the final finishing will be.

Rub a new file with chalk to prevent it clogging. When the file becomes clogged, clean it by rubbing a piece of wood across the cuts, or use a piece of brass if it is heavily clogged. A new file should first be used on precious or non-ferrous metals like copper or brass as steel will damage it.

Files should be kept separate from one another and other tools to prevent the teeth from being damaged. Sheaths can be made for the larger files by wrapping cardboard loosely round the file and then wrapping tape round the cardboard. A magnetic strip is a convenient way of keeping the smaller files apart.

Below is a list of other types of files that you will come across:

Gapping files These are round, parallel files and are used mainly for filing a groove to take a hinge.

Parallel files These are flat files which have half-round edges that do the cutting. The sides of these files are completely smooth.

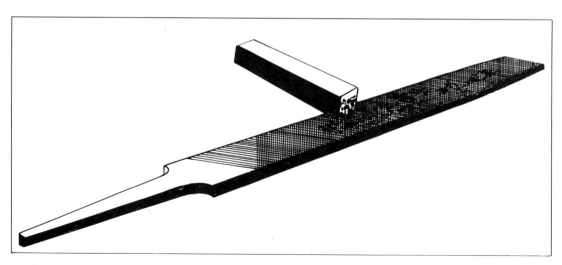

Unclogging a clogged file with a piece of brass or copper. A file will not cut properly if it is clogged.

Slotting files These are like parallel files, but they are a lot thinner and are used to cut slots in screw heads.

Escapement files These are the same as needle files, but are smaller and only come in a fine cut.

Riffler files These files are available in two sizes and have different shaped ends. They are used for awkward corners and areas that are not accessible for normal files.

PLIERS

Pliers are used for holding and bending metal. They are identified by the shape of their jaw, and you should always choose a pair with a box joint rather than a lap joint as the latter will wobble with use. The jaws should be smooth so as not to mark the metal.

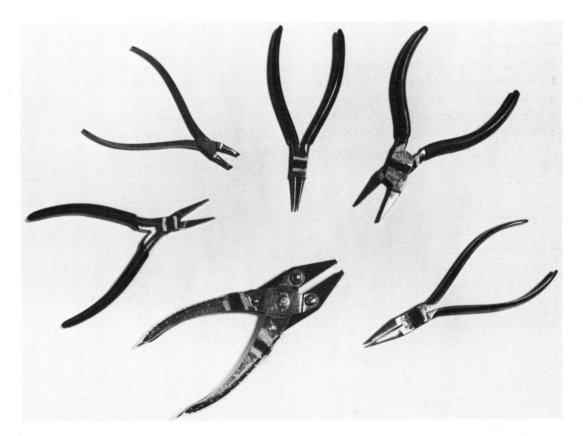

Pliers, from left to right: well machined flat-nose pliers; an old pair of round-nose pliers with the ends bent up at right angles; a pair of fine round-nose pliers; half-round pliers; and an ordinary pair of flat-nose pliers. Centre: a pair of parallel pliers.

Round-nose pliers

These are round in shape and taper to their ends. They are used to bend and shape objects that need to be round or curved.

Half-round pliers

These have one surface which is flat and one which is half-round, and are used to bend the metal into a circular shape as for a ring.

Flat-nose pliers

These are mainly used for gripping work that would be too small to hold in the hand. They are also ideal for opening jump rings.

Parallel pliers

These have jaws that open parallel to each other and are excellent for straightening out metal and for holding work securely while filing.

Bending a strip of sheet round on its edge. Use half-round pliers to hold the strip on either edge to bend the metal, and flat pliers to hold it top and bottom. In the background is a rack holding an assortment of pliers.

As well as using pliers independently, they can be used in pairs. To bend a flat piece of metal at right angles you will need half-round and flat pliers. Hold the metal with the flat pliers. Place the half-round pliers on either side of the metal with the curved jaw on the side that is to be bent, and then twist the half-round pliers to bend the metal.

A slot cut with a hack-saw into the inside of each jaw of the half-round pliers and equidistant from each end, will help to hold the work secure when bending it. Old or inexpensive pliers can be filed and shaped for different uses, such as for holding collets.

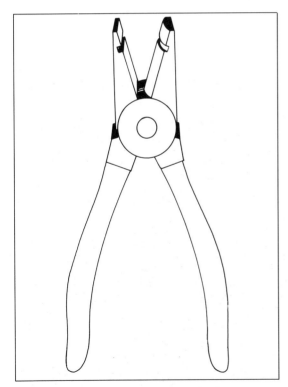

A close-up of the slots that can be cut on the inside of a pair of half-round pliers to hold strips of metal by their edges while they are being bent.

OTHER HAND TOOLS

You will need many other tools; these are listed below:

Metal ruler The metal ruler is used for marking out and drawing straight lines that are not right angles. All measurements in jewellery are in millimetres because they are so small – inches are very rarely used. The ruler should be 15cm (6in) long and marked in inches and millimetres.

Square This is used to check that corners are exactly 90°. The square should be treated with care and kept where it won't be knocked by other tools or accidently dropped on the floor.

Scriber The scriber is used to mark out designs on the metal.

Centre punch The centre punch is used to make a round indentation in the metal. It is held over the spot where the hole is to be drilled and is tapped with a hammer.

Burnisher This is a smooth length of steel used for polishing corners. It is useful when setting stones as it leaves a polish on the metal. Burnishers can also have a stoned finish – these are used as very fine files.

Dividers These are like compasses and can be set to any width. They are used to mark parallel lines and circles, and are also used for marking off set distances.

Shears These are used for cutting metal and for cutting solder into very small pieces known as paillons. They can be either straight or curved. The action of the shears will distort the edge of the metal, so they should not be used where an edge is to be soldered. A saw should be used in this case as it will cut cleanly leaving only a few burrs which can be removed with a file.

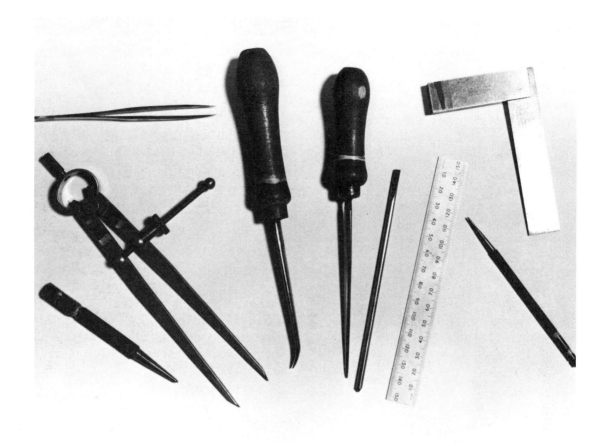

From left to right: a centre punch; a large pair of dividers; a pair of tweezers suitable for placing paillons of solder; two burnishers, one straight and one curved; a homemade flat-ended scriber/centre cutter; a 15mm metal ruler; a pointed-end scriber and lastly, in the top right-hand corner, a square.

Side-cutter These are used to cut wire, and because of their shape they can cut very close to the work.

Tweezers Tweezers are used to hold and pick up pieces of metal that are to be soldered or that are too hot to pick up with your fingers. A pair of self-locking tweezers are most suitable for soldering as they hold work without needing to be held themselves. Use a pair of fine tweezers for picking up and placing paillons of solder or other small items.

Borax dish This is a round porcelain dish used for mixing and grinding borax.

Soldering torch This is used to solder metal together.

Rawhide mallet A rawhide mallet is used to flatten and hammer out metal without damaging its surface.

Small ball-pein hammer This is used for shaping and hammering out metal and also for tapping punches.

Riveting hammer This is small hammer that is used for riveting and for light, delicate work.

Planishing hammer This hammer has

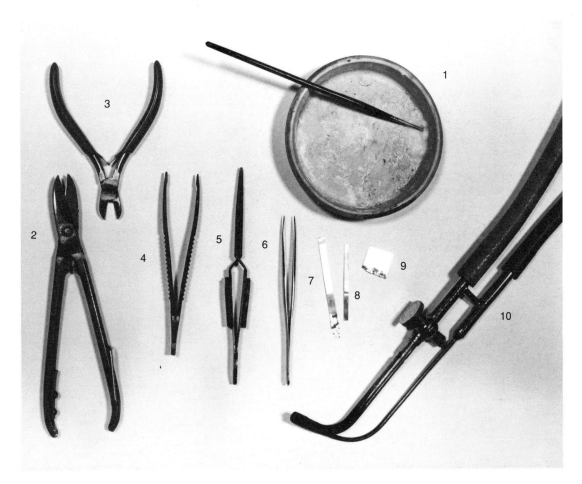

1   A borax dish and borax brush; 2   A pair of shears for cutting sheet metal;
3   A pair of side-cutters for cutting wire; 4   A pair of plastic tweezers for using
in the pickle; 5   A pair of self-locking tweezers with heat-resistant pads; 6   A
pair of soldering tweezers; 7   A strip of hard solder, with some paillons cut off
the end; 8   A strip of easy solder; 9   A strip of gold solder; 10   A mouth-blown
soldering torch.

square and round faces on its head that
are finished to a high polish. These faces
will leave a polished finish on metal and
must be kept where the heads will not be
marked, as these marks will be transmitted
to the metal when the hammer is used.
Hand drill   This is a small chuck fixed to
a round handle that will rotate independently of the chuck. It comes with two
interchangeable chucks and will hold

twist drills of up to 2.5mm. It is turned
with your fingers and the handle is held
in the palm of your hand.

When using a hand drill make sure the
drill bits fit comfortably into the chosen
chuck. The drill should be held vertically
over the hole made by the centre punch.
Twist drills (drill bits)   These do the actual cutting and will fit into all types of
drill. They come in a wide range of sizes.

29

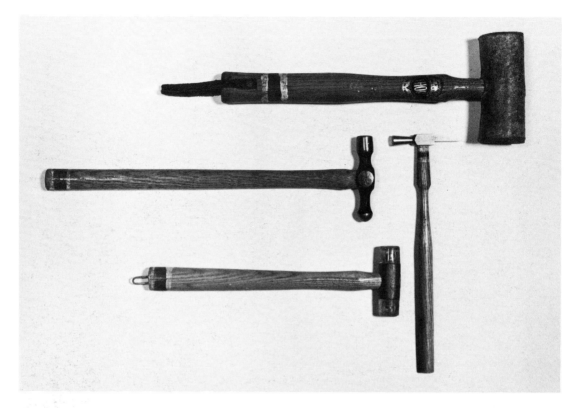

The three horizontal hammers from top to bottom are: a rawhide mallet; a general-purpose ball-pein hammer; a nylon-headed mallet. The vertical hammer is a watch-maker's, or riveting hammer.

Small drills can be made from needles after their heads have been broken off and their ends stoned to form a cutting end.

Bow drill The drill works by twisting the string around the shaft using the wooden bar. While holding the bar and the flywheel still, place the drill over the spot where the hole is to be made. Release the flywheel and pull gently down on the bar, releasing pressure on the bar just before it reaches the bottom, thus allowing the string to re-wind back up the shaft. Continue in this manner until the hole is complete. This will become easier with practice. A little oil on the drill bit will assist in cutting the metal. The bow drill also comes with different sized chucks.

Pin vice This is an open-ended chuck used for holding wire or tube when cutting or filing, and can be obtained in various sizes. Ones with square ends are better as they can be used as a reference when filing something into a square. Pin vices are also used to hold drills and broachers (*see* below). Pin clamps hold small pieces of metal together for filing, sawing and drilling.

Broachers These are like round needle files but are pentagonal with smooth edges and come in a large range of sizes from 0.1mm to 1cm. Broachers are used to open out holes and to taper them for hinges. They will also burnish a hole to help it resist wear.

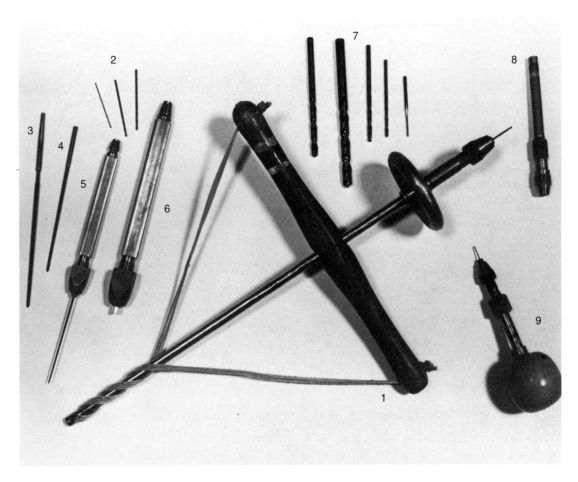

1 A bow drill; 2 Small drill bits; 3 A medium-sized broacher; 4 A small-sized broacher; 5 A small square chucked pin vice holding a broacher and with interchangeable collets; 6 A large square chucked pin vice holding some wire and with interchangeable collets; 7 Five assorted drill bits; 8 A round chucked pin vice with fixed collet. 9 A small hand-held drill holding a small drill bit and with a rotating handle.

Verniers and micrometers These are precision measuring instruments. Verniers will measure the outside, inside and depth of an object to within 0.1mm. The vernier has a slide which is marked in millimetres and inches, some also have a dial which is marked in either millimetres or inches. The slide is moved up and down by a wheel to close on the work and the measurement is read off the slide or

the dial. A micrometer is for much finer measurements (to within 0.001mm) and is used for measuring the thickness of the metal. The measurements are read from the screw end which adjusts the measuring arms. This is a delicate instrument and should be handled with care.

Micrometers give either metric or imperial measurements whereas verniers generally give both.

31

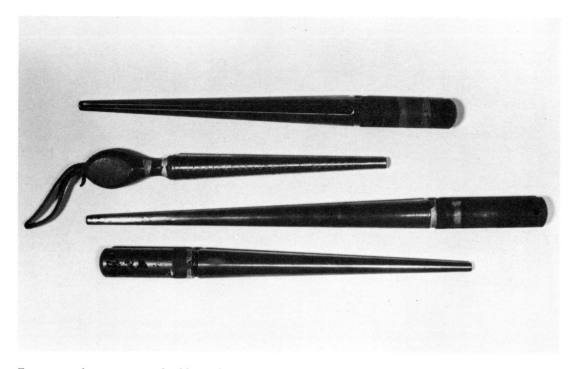

From top to bottom: a round triblet with a groove along its length; a ring size stick; a round-ring triblet; a shorter round-ring triblet.

Ring mandrel or triblet This is a long, tapered, polished rod and is used for rounding up the shank of a ring or slightly enlarging it, and for holding the ring if you are making a textured surface.

Triblets come in different sizes for making collets, rings, bracelets and boxes. They can be round, round with a groove, square or oval in shape.

Ring stick This is a tapered tube used to measure the size of a ring. Rings can be slipped on to the ring stick to measure their size, or to check that they are the right size. The ring stick is marked in the same way as ring sizes (*see* below), but also has half-sizes between the letters.

Ring sizes These are a series of holes stamped out of metal or plastic that correspond to the sizes marked on the ring stick. They are slipped over the knuckle of a finger to measure its size for a ring. There are twenty-six graduated rings marked A–Z for reference.

Gravers and scorpers These are various shaped steel cutting tools used for carving, engraving, setting and texturing. They come in about a dozen different shapes, each shape having five or six sizes.

Draw-plates and draw-tongs Draw-plates are steel plates with diminishing holes of various shapes. When wire is pulled through, it is squeezed to the size of the hole. The wire is first filed to a point at one end and then placed in the back of the hole. It is held in position by a pair of draw-tongs and is then pulled through. The wire will become work-hardened (*see* Glossary) after being pulled through two or three holes and will need to be an-

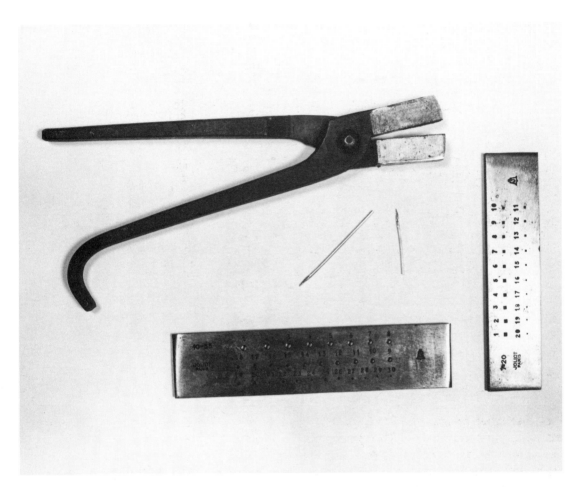

Top, a pair of draw tongs; bottom, a round-holed draw plate; right, a square-holed draw plate; centre, two pieces of drawn wire.

nealed. Each shape has about twenty holes so that the wire can be reduced by about 2mm.

Swage-block These are used for making tubing and shaping metal. They come in various sizes.

Eyeglass A 7.5cm focal length aluminium eyeglass is useful when engraving or when doing close work.

Soldering block These are made of a fire-resistant compound and can be bought as flat mats or as small blocks 7.5cm by 12.5cm.

Charcoal block This is of the same size as the soldering block and, although it is expensive, it is good for soldering small items. Care must be taken after soldering to ensure that the block is not smoldering as it will quickly burn away. It is advisable to cover the bottom half of the block with plaster of Paris or investment plaster. This will help prevent the block from splitting into pieces and will hold it together. Try not to allow the block to become damp – if it does it must be heated up slowly or it will split.

33

A doming block and punches with a lead-forming block (top centre).

Doming block and punches A doming block is a brass or steel block containing polished concave hollows of diminishing sizes. The punches are made of steel or box wood and have a turned ball at one end (this is polished on steel punches).

The doming block and punches are used to convert a flat metal disc into a dome. Punches range in size from 2mm to 20mm, each dome increasing by 0.5mm.

A block of lead is useful for doming metal that is an odd shape – as lead is one of the softest metals it will give way as it is hammered.

Punches These are lengths of steel which have either a patterned or shaped end. They are tapped at the opposite end to leave the pattern in the metal. They are mainly used for chasing and repoussé.

Taps, dies and screw-plates These are used to cut screw-threads. The taps are used to cut a thread on the inside of a hole and come in threes. The first tap used is a starting tap and the first portion of this tap is not threaded but tapered. The second tap has a slight taper on the bottom and the remainder is threaded. The third tap has threads along its whole length and

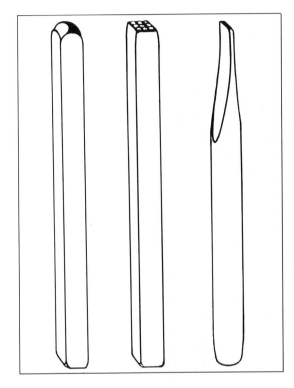

Three different types of punches: left, a domed and polished end; centre, a textured end; right, a chisel-shaped punch.

is often called a plug tap. This third tap is used to cut a thread to the bottom of a blind hole. The hole that is to be threaded is drilled out to the core diameter of the tap. The tap is twisted into the hole to cut the thread.

Dies are used to cut the thread on the outside of wire and they are placed in a special holder. The size of the die can be altered very slightly. After one cut has been made through the die, it is closed up slightly and passed through the die again to clean the thread up.

A screw-plate is a series of ten dies that are all on one sheet of metal. These cannot be adjusted like dies and they come with their own corresponding taps. The threads they make are unique to that particular make of screw-plate.

Taps and dies are available in imperial or metric sizes. Imperial taps and dies are measured from 0B.A. down to 12B.A. Very small watch-makers' taps and dies are measured metrically and start at 1mm and go down in size to about 0.4mm.

3 Metals

All metals used in jewellery making contain three qualities in varying degrees. These are:

Tenacity This is a property in the material which resists fracture under tension.
Ductility This is the property which allows a substance to be drawn out without fracture. Gold is the most ductile metal – 1g can be drawn down to become 2 miles long.
Malleability This is the property which enables a material to be spread under impact without fracture. Gold and silver have excellent malleability. Gold can be spread out until it is only four millionths of an inch thick.

Precious metals in their pure state are very vulnerable to wear and damage as they are so soft. Therefore, for jewellery making they are hardened by combining with another metal to make an alloy. Precious metals are also alloyed to give different colour variations.

You will have to purchase your precious metal from a bullion merchant, but you should be able to find non-precious metals locally – your local scrap-yard is often a good place to look, although the quality may not always be what you are looking for.

Some metals are not compatable with each other. Lead and aluminium will eat into silver when it is heated up, leaving holes in the work. For this reason different files should be used when working on silver and aluminium. Silver has the same effect on platinum.

PRECIOUS METALS

Silver

Silver is the most commonly found precious metal and is therefore the least expensive and most frequently used. Silver is a white-coloured metal and is alloyed with copper. This gives it more strength and hardness so that it is easier to work with, and forms an alloy with a silver content of 92.5 per cent which is called standard or sterling silver. There is also a higher standard of silver called Britannia, which was used mainly for coins and which is too soft for jewellery. Fine or pure silver can be bought and is ideal for making bezels when setting stones.

When silver is heated up for annealing or soldering, some of the copper comes to the surface and leaves a purple stain on the metal called fire-stain. This is overcome commercially by plating, but it can be removed by using Water of Ayr stone (a form of slate) dipped in water or by filing. There are chemicals that will inhibit fire-stain and these will be mentioned later.

Gold

Gold is the most beautiful and valuable of metals. It is non-magnetic and does not corrode. It is the most desirable metal used in jewellery, either in its own right or as gold plate. Pure gold is too soft for jewellery if it is to be robust and not wear, so it is alloyed with either copper, silver or zinc to produce harder and cheaper alloys of varying colours. The alloys of gold are graded by an old system called carat which is based and proportioned on 24 carats of pure gold. It is alloyed in proportions of 22, 18, 14 or 9 carats, indicating the amount of gold in each alloy. For example, 18 carat gold will contain eighteen parts of gold with six parts of base metal or silver. 9 carat is the cheapest and is brown in colour, and is also the hardest as it contains the largest proportion of base metal. 14 carat gold is mainly used overseas and is often the minimum legal gold alloy. 18 carat has a warm gold colour, and is slightly harder to work than silver but considerably stronger.

Gold is also alloyed with other metals to form white gold which is the same colour as silver. Other tints can be obtained by adding different metals in the alloy, for example, silver gives a green tint and copper a reddish gold tint.

Platinum

Platinum is a tough, white metal of high density with a high melting point. It is malleable and ductile and will take a high polish, but it is very expensive. It is mainly used in catalytic converters for car exhausts, but is also used in jewellery, particularly for the setting of diamonds as it will keep a high polish when soldered. Although it is a hard metal, it is slow to work-harden. Because of its high melting point specialist soldering torches are required.

NON-FERROUS METALS

Non-ferrous metals, or base metals, are the most likely metals to be used by the beginner. They are cheaper to use than precious metals and have a wider range of colours. They have almost the same working qualities as precious metals, are readily available and can be soldered with silver solder. Base metals are all an alloy of copper.

Copper

Copper is a reddish, soft ductile metal with good electrical conductivity. It has similar working qualities to silver and it is the softest of all of the base metals.

Brass

The most popular copper alloy is brass, which is yellow and is made by alloying copper with zinc. There are two types of brass – alpha and alpha-beta, the latter being used mainly for castings. Alpha brass is used in jewellery as it is strong and ductile but is also hard working. An easier working brass known as free-cutting brass is used for turned components. This type of brass contains lead which will make it easier to cut, and it also contains zinc.

Guilding Metal

Guilding metal is a type of brass which contains more copper than brass and has a warm reddish-yellow colour similar to gold. Guilding metal is a ductile metal and is mainly used for hollow vessels – these vessels are then plated, hence its name.

Nickel

Nickel is also a type of brass but contains nickel as well as copper and zinc. It is also known as nickel silver or German silver as although it contains no silver it is the same colour as silver. It is a tough, ductile alloy that is slightly harder to work than brass but will not tarnish as easily as the other metals.

Titanium

This is a hard metal and cannot be soldered to other metals because of its high melting point. It is mainly used for the variety of colours that can be obtained by anodizing the metal. By passing different currents through the titanium, which oxidize the surface, it is possible to achieve a wide range of colours varying from purple through to greenish-yellow and blue. The colours will be more vibrant if the titanium is first etched in hydrofluoric acid, but this must be used with extreme caution.

Aluminium

Aluminium can also be anodized. This will not colour the metal but will cause a pitted surface which will hold coloured dyes. These dyes can then be fixed by holding the metal in steam from a kettle.

Tin

Tin is a soft crystalline metal which is seldom used in jewellery. It does provide an excellent contrast to gold but will prevent the gold from being hallmarked.

Monel

Monel is mainly used in jewellery for making springs as it is a hard metal. It is an alloy of copper and has a slightly purple colour when matt.

FERROUS METALS

Ferrous metals contain iron and usually consist of iron or different types of steel. They are rarely used in fine jewellery but are found in contemporary jewellery, either as part of the piece or for the pin.

Steel

Mild steel is the most commonly used ferrous metal. It must be absolutely clean before it is soldered or the solder will not flow. Steel comes in many forms which are all of a similar colour.

Carbon steel can be hardened depending on the content of carbon. Carbon steel with a carbon content of 0.9 per cent to 1.1 per cent, known as silver steel because of its appearance, is a general steel suitable for all types of components that need to be hardened and tempered. The steel is hardened by heating it up to a cherry red and then quenching it in water. It is then cleaned and slowly heated up to one of the temper colours which range from pale straw to light blue. When the steel reaches light blue it becomes soft again. When the desired colour is reached, it is removed from the heat and allowed to cool.

HALLMARKING AND ASSAYING

Hallmarking dates back to 1300 when a statute by Edward I instituted the system.

STANDARD MARK

British articles

prior to 1975	Standard	From 1975
	22 carat gold marked in England / marked in Scotland	916
	18 carat gold marked in England / marked in Scotland	750
	14 carat gold	585
	9 carat gold	375
	sterling silver marked in England / marked in Scotland	
	Britannia silver	
—	platinum	

Imported Articles

prior to 1975		From 1975
	22 carat gold	916
	18 carat gold	750
	14 carat gold	585
	9 carat gold	375
	sterling silver	925
	Britannia silver	958
—	platinum	950

ASSAY OFFICE MARK

British articles

prior to 1975	Assay Office	From 1975
gold and sterling silver / Britannia silver	London	gold, silver and platinum
gold / silver	Birmingham	gold and platinum / silver
gold / silver	Sheffield	gold, silver and platinum
gold and silver	Edinburgh	gold, silver and platinum

Imported Articles

prior to 1975	Assay Office	From 1975
gold	London	gold and silver / platinum — unchanged
	Birmingham	unchanged
	Sheffield	unchanged
	Edinburgh	unchanged

A complete British hallmark showing the symbols from which it is composed.

It was introduced to protect the public against fraud and the trader against unfair competition. All items of jewellery made from precious metals must be hallmarked before they can be sold. For an item to be marked it must be of a certain level of pureness or over. Gold has four standards of purity – 9, 14, 18 and 22 carat. For silver the minimum standards are 92.5 per cent for sterling and 95.84 per cent for Britannia. For platinum the minimum standard is 95 per cent platinum.

An article may not be called gold, silver or platinum unless it is hallmarked or exempt. If an item contains both gold and silver it is hallmarked as silver. Gold and platinum articles can be hallmarked as separate metals, and if the total gold content of the piece is less than 50 per cent of the total weight, the gold must be 18 carat. The platinum will carry a full mark and the gold will carry an 18 carat part mark which is the 18 carat mark and the centre mark (the Assay Office mark).

An article of precious metal will not be marked if it falls below the minimum standard, or if a base metal is fixed to it either by soldering or riveting, unless the base metal is being used for a function for which a precious metal would be too weak, such as a spring for snaps or pins for brooches. If you are in any doubt it is advisable to check with the Assay Office first and they will advise you as to whether it will be possible to hallmark the piece if you are including base metal in this way.

A hallmark is made up of four parts. First is the maker's or sponsor's mark, which comprises the initials of the maker or company that made the piece. Next comes the standard mark which will have one of seven marks for the different metals and standards of purity. Next comes the Assay Office mark, and last of all the date letter which changes every year. There are also international convention marks which are applied to some imported articles.

4 Soldering

Soldering is the main method for attaching one piece of metal to another, making a strong invisible join. Carried out correctly and with the right processes it is a simple operation. As with most things it will become easier with practice, and only experience will tell you how many joints can be soldered with one hardness of solder or just how hot the metal must be for the solder to run.

The pieces of metal are attached by flowing another piece of molten metal between them, which makes a permanent join on cooling. The molten metal used to join the two pieces is called solder and is the same type of alloy as the work being soldered. It is a lower quality alloy, so it will have a lower melting point, and this allows the solder to melt without also melting the metal it is joining. The solder penetrates the surfaces of the joining metal to fuse the edges together. The strongest join is made by using a solder with only a slightly lower melting point than the metal. If there is too great a reduction in the quality of the alloy it may affect the assay test, and too much solder could prevent it from being hallmarked. To prevent this happening, the edges must fit flush before soldering, so that the solder is used to join them and not to fill any gaps.

Any excess solder will need to be filed away after all the soldering operations have been completed and before the work is sent off to be assayed. If this is not done, it could affect the sample taken from the work.

SOLDERING TORCHES

Soldering torches run on a mixture of gas and air, and if a higher temperature is required then a combination of gas and oxygen or oxygen and hydrogen should be used. All torches are of similar design having one nozzle which, on some models, can be interchanged with other nozzles of various sizes. The torch has a handle with a tap which is used to vary the amount of gas and therefore the size of the flame. On some models there is a second tap to control the amount of air or oxygen being used so that the flame can be made hotter or softer, although sometimes one tap does both these functions. There are also one or two connections for different tubing if bottled gas is used, and this piping must be secured with a jubilee clip.

Some torches just screw on to the top of a compressed can of gas. These are fine for occasional soldering, but are very awkward to use as they need to be held more or less upright to allow the gas to vapourize, whereas the ideal position when working is to have the flame pointing down at the work – usually flat on the bench. You will also find it difficult to adjust the flame while working as you will have to do it with the hand which is already holding the can as your other hand will be holding the work.

The two types of torch that are most suitable run off mains or bottled gas, one type using compressed air and the other using mouth-blown air.

A soldering torch which runs off natural gas and compressed air. This and a mouth-blown air torch are the two most likely to be used.

Compressed Air Torch

Torches using compressed air are available with different sized nozzles. Large nozzles are mainly used for annealing large pieces of work and melting metal. Medium nozzles are ideal for annealing and soldering larger items of silver. Small nozzles are most likely to be used by the jeweller, as a small, fine, hard flame can be achieved with this torch that is ideal for soldering small items together quickly, such as jump rings. However, care must be taken when using hard solder as you may melt the metal. The hardness or fierceness of the flame can be altered by adjusting the amount of air used, and the size of the flame can be changed by adjusting the amount of gas. You must remember that if you wish to increase the size of the flame but retain its intensity, you must also increase the flow of air.

The hottest part of the flame is the tip of the inner blue cone and this is the part that is used when soldering. The centre of this cone is the coolest part of the flame which is also cooler towards its end. This type of torch will, of course, need a compressor to provide the air and is therefore best suited to workshops which carry out a lot of solder work and have other equipment that runs off compressed air, such as sand-blasters and air-powered grinders and burrs.

Mouth-Blown Torch

Mouth-blown torches are most common in small workshops, and will run off the mains gas supply or bottled gas such as propane. The flame produced by this type of torch cannot be made as fine or as hard as a gas air torch, but the softer flame it produces will heat the metal more evenly and is good for general soldering. It is very easy to adjust the amount of gas as there is only one adjusting tap. This enables you to make the flame finer, harder, bigger or softer as required while soldering a join.

Do not be alarmed if you seem to be using a lot of breath at first, as you will soon be able to regulate your breathing. A slight difference in the flame can be achieved by blowing harder or softer. With practice you will find your own natural rate of blowing so that the flame will last quite a long time between breaths. Some people can even manage to breathe in through their nose while still blowing out through their mouth into the torch.

If you find a mouth-blown torch too difficult, an air pump from a fish tank or a foot pump can be used instead. It is also possible to buy small hand-held torches that run off 2.5kg bottles of gas and which give a fine flame similar to that of a gas air torch. However, the flame will not be as hard or fierce.

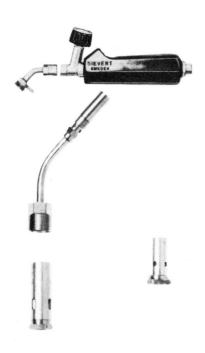

This soldering torch is designed to run off bottled gas. Also shown are two of the interchangeable nozzles or burners that are available for this torch.

Other Torches

There are two types of soldering torch that you are not likely to use. One is the micro weld. This produces its own gas by electrolysis from distilled water. It produces a very fine flame with no side heat which makes it possible to solder very complicated work in precious metals that would be technically impossible using conventional methods. The other torch uses a mixture of oxygen and natural gas. This mixture will produce a hot flame but not as fine as the micro weld flame. It is used on the same high-melting point metals such as white gold and platinum.

Safety

When using a soldering torch always remember to turn off the gas at the end of the day or when it is not required again. Always check that the gas is turned off at the mains or at the bottle before you leave the workshop.

TYPES OF SOLDER

Soft Solder

Soft solder melts at a low temperature and is only used on repair work where hard solder would be impractical, for example, when repairing a stone setting which cannot be removed but which would be damaged by the heat needed for hard solder. Where soft solder has been used on precious metals, the metal must be cleaned thoroughly after soldering or the lead in the solder will eat into it.

Hard Solder

Hard solders are most commonly used and contain no lead. The solder used on silver is made up of silver, copper and zinc, and this solder is also used for base metals. The purity of silver solder has to be sufficient to pass the hallmarking standard. There are also gold and platinum hard solders to use on the respective metals. There is no reason why a higher quality gold cannot be used to solder a lower quality gold, for example, 22ct gold can be used to solder 18ct gold. The higher melting point of platinum and white gold requires a gas–oxygen mix to melt the solder. Platinum solder does not need to be soldered with a flux except for 'extra easy', but putting some water or

43

flux on the paillons will help to hold them to the join and prevent them being blown away by the flame from the torch. With hard solders the high melting point results in an oxide forming on the components being soldered. Therefore, a flux is used so that the melting solder can fuse to a clean metal surface (*see* below).

Buying Solder

Silver and gold hard solders are available in a range of melting temperatures known as 'easy', 'medium' and 'hard'. Platinum solder also has an 'extra easy' and 'medium hard'. The extra easy solder tends to have a slightly yellow tint to it because of the gold it contains.

Silver solder comes in flat wire form of different widths and thicknesses depending on the solder, hard solder being the widest and medium the narrowest but deepest. Easy is the same thickness as the hard solder but not as wide. Silver solder can be bought in any length that is required.

Gold and platinum solders come in thin rectangles 2g in weight and are stamped with the carat and type of solder, for example, hard, medium or easy.

PREPARING THE SOLDER

The solder is cut up into paillons initially. These are small squares of solder and are formed by cutting up the strips or rectangles of solder into thinner new strips and then cutting across these to make small squares as required for each soldering job. If you are using solder regularly, the paillons can be cut straight into a small container to give several days' supply. If you are only soldering occasionally it is better to cut them as required as it is essential that they are kept clean. It is much easier to clean a large strip with emery paper than each individual paillon.

In practice you may find that the silver solder strips are too thick to cut into practical-sized paillons that do not leave a lot of extra solder on the join. If this is the case the strips can be rolled thinner in a rolling mill first. Only a small amount at a time should be rolled out as solder cannot be annealed. Mark the strips when they are fully rolled out so that they are readily identified as hard, medium or easy. The same applies to any containers that hold solder paillons. There is nothing worse than using a paillon to solder a joint only to find that it comes undone when you solder another joint because easy was mistaken for hard, or the other way around.

Before placing the paillons in position for soldering, dip them in some flux (*see* below). This will prevent the paillon from oxidizing and will help hold it in place over the joint which is to be soldered. When soldering large joints in silver it is sometimes easier to use the solder in a strip. The same process is used as when using paillons, but the solder must not be heated up. It is only attached to the joint when the joint is at the correct heat to melt the solder – this then runs into the joint.

FLUXES

Fluxes are applied to the metal before the metal is heated up for soldering. Fluxes for soft solder are based on resin and are sometimes incorporated in the solder. Fluxes for hard solder are based on borax and are available as straight borax powder or as a cone that is ground up with water to a creamy consistency. There are flux powders based on borax for each solder and all are mixed to a cream with water. A liquid easy-flow flux is also available.

Fluxes are applied over the joint before heating. The joint is then heated so that the water in the flux evaporates. The paillons are placed over the joint after the water has evaporated – placing them over before the water has evaporated could cause them to dislodge. The flux prevents oxidization, leaving a clean joint for the solder to fuse the metal together.

When using silver, argo-tect can be applied after some flux has been applied. Argo-tect is a mixture of chemicals in powder form which is mixed with methylated spirit to the same consistency as the flux. It is painted over the whole piece which is being soldered, and helps inhibit fire-stain. It also contains a flux, although I find it a good idea to apply more flux separately as well. The argo-tect will boil up more than the borax so it is best to boil off the methylated spirit before placing the solder.

SETTING UP THE WORK FOR SOLDERING

The work should be placed as securely as possible on a block, with the joint or joints that are going to be soldered easily accessible from one point. The placement of the work depends entirely on what type of joint you are soldering. Common sense, and in some cases balance, will decide the position.

There are two main forms of joint, the most commonly used being the butt joint where the two pieces are placed end to end, or alternatively where one piece butts against the side of the other piece.

The second type of joint is where two pieces are soldered one on top of the other, the top piece of metal having a bevel filed round its edge. Paillons of solder and borax are evenly placed over the top component and heated until they run over the surface of the metal. It is then cleaned in pickle and filed flat so that there are no high points of solder. The top component is then boraxed and placed solder-side down on top of the bottom piece of metal, and heated up until the solder runs around the edges. The bevel prevents the solder from running all over the bottom piece of metal.

It is possible to use a quicker method for this second joint but it is not as strong. The solder is not run on one piece first but is sandwiched in the middle with the borax and then heated up until the solder runs. The top piece will close on to the bottom as the solder runs, but it may need a push and oxide could remain in the middle.

An item may have one or several joints. Where there are several joints to solder it is advisable to do as many as possible at one go using hard solder. When you cannot use the hard solder any longer, because the heat required is affecting the other joints, use medium solder. If easy solder has not been used when a piece is made, it can safely be used if a repair is needed without fear of unsoldering other joints. If a piece requires several solder joints it is as well to add a little more solder than usual as some will burn off when the next joint is heated up to the same temperature. Do not clean up the joints until you have soldered them all, unless another piece has to fit over a joint thus making it very difficult to clean when all the soldering is finished.

SOLDERING BLOCKS

There are two types of solder blocks that can be used. The most popular one is a charcoal block as it does not absorb as much heat as a fire-resistant block. Charcoal blocks are expensive and as they absorb moisture they must be kept warm or else heated up slowly to evaporate the moisture, otherwise the block will split up. Binding wire can be wrapped around the block to help hold it together or, alternatively, the bottom and most of the sides can be covered with plaster of Paris or investment plaster. If the charcoal block still glows red after soldering, extinguish with a little water or the block will burn away. The block can be filed flat with a coarse file or coarse emery paper. Metal can be pushed into the block and pieces of charcoal taken out so that the piece to be soldered fits comfortably.

Fire-resistant blocks are used with large items, because the extreme heat used could burn most of a charcoal block away.

Both of the blocks should be placed on a fire-resistant mat which will protect the bench. It is also useful to place some pieces of broken-up fire-bricks around a large item to reflect the heat. Some work will need to be held in place with binding wire. The binding wire should be doubled over with a loop and then a twist made at the corners. This can then be tightened when both ends of the wire are secured. Binding wire must be removed before going into the pickle.

SOLDERING

Start by making absolutely certain that both parts to be joined are clean and will make a close joint, as the solder will not fill gaps. If the piece has become work-hardened it must be annealed first and thoroughly cleaned or the joint will open up as the metal softens with the heat.

1. Paint flux over and around the joint, and argo-tect all over the piece if it is silver.
2. Heat up the piece until the water in the borax has boiled off.
3. Place the paillons to the joint after dipping them in the borax.
4. Slowly heat all around so the piece heats up evenly until the solder runs. It will form a ball just before it flows along the joint, and you should remove the flame immediately.
5. Allow the piece to cool slightly and then place it in the pickle to clean off the oxide and flux.

ANNEALING

Annealing softens metal when it has become work-hardened. Filing, hammering and bending of the metal will cause the molecules in the metal to become compressed and brittle. Annealing allows the molecules to return to their natural form. It is done by heating the metal up to a cherry red and then quenching it in water. You should then place the metal in the pickle to clean it and dry it thoroughly. The metal can also be allowed to cool naturally. With silver, unless it is painted with argo-tect, do not heat it quite as far as cherry red and do not keep it at this heat for very long to reduce the amount of fire-stain.

Filing and bending metal does not work-harden it as much as hammering, rolling and drawing down. Two or three

Paillons being placed on to a joint which is to be soldered, using tweezers. The work has been set up on a charcoal block which has plaster of Paris round its sides and base. The charcoal block sits on a fire-brick which is placed on a fire-resistant mat.

The flame can just be discerned heating up the work after the paillons have been placed. The tweezers are held ready to push the work, or a paillon of solder, back into place if they move while being soldered.

47

passes through the rollers is, on average, all you can do without annealing – more if the metal is thin and less if it is thick. It will become more difficult to roll through as it becomes harder and will then need to be annealed. Thick wire that is being drawn down or wire that is being drawn through a different shaped hole will have to be annealed every time. Thin wire will probably go through three holes between annealing. The wire will become hard to pull and hot when it is work-hardened. Different metals become work-hardened at different rates – brass, for instance, will work-harden at a quicker rate than gold.

PICKLES

The main pickle solution is made up using 10 per cent sulphuric acid and 90 per cent water. This solution is kept in a heat-resistant glass dish or a lead container and is placed on a fire-resistant gauze mat on a tripod. It is then heated using a Bunsen burner which is set to burn with a low flame. Do not boil off all the water and when it has boiled almost dry, let the solution cool down and slowly pour it into some more water. *Never* do it the other way round as it could cause an explosion.

ALWAYS ADD ACID 'A' TO WATER 'W'. Remember it alphabetically – A to W. The same applies when mixing up a new solution – acid to water. You should also be careful not to splash the pickle solution on to your clothes as it will leave a hole after washing.

After the work has become clean in the pickle, take it out, wash it thoroughly under a running tap and then dry it well to prevent the tools from becoming rusty.

Another form of pickle is alum mixed with water. It is safer than the sulphuric acid pickle but must be at boiling point to clean the work well and may take a little longer than the acid.

NEVER USE IRON OR STEEL TWEEZERS OR TONGS TO TAKE OUT OR PUT WORK INTO EITHER OF THESE PICKLES. It will turn your work pink and it is hard to remove especially in awkward corners. The acid reacts with iron and steel to form a copper solution which is then plated on to base and noble metals, so you should use only base metal or plastic tweezers and tongs with the pickles.

There are also safety pickles that help remove fire-stain from silver, but as with alum they need to be used when they are hot.

5 Polishing

Apart from stone setting, polishing is the final process and is visually the most important. It is, therefore, essential that great care is taken at this stage to bring out the very best in your work with a good polish. A highly polished finish will contrast well with a matt finish and an unblemished polish will enhance your design. Careless polishing that has rounded corners or edges will, however good the shine, alter the visual impression of the work and weaken the design. Obtaining a perfect polish can be a slow and repetitive process, but the end result will make it all worth while.

Polishing is a process which reduces the size of surface scratches until they become indistinguishable to the eye. This is achieved by using coated papers and a polishing compound on the mops of your polisher.

POLISHING PAPERS AND STONES

Emery Paper

The main coated paper used is emery paper. Emery is made from natural earth and is a very abrasive material. It is graded into different grit sizes – the finest grade is crocus and this is followed by grades 4/0, 3/0, 2/0, 1/0, 1, 2, and 3, with grade 3 being the coarsest.

To ensure that the edges of your work are kept sharp when polishing flat surfaces, the paper should be fixed to a flat surface or on to a piece of plate glass. When polishing curved or inaccessible areas, the emery paper can be wrapped around a buff stick. You will need to score the paper slightly to ensure a snug fit around the stick. Buff sticks come in many shapes but the most commonly used ones are flat, round, triangular and half-round. Sometimes you will find it necessary to fold the emery paper double and use it without a rigid support.

This cuff-link was polished before it should have been to demonstrate what a bad polish looks like. As you can see, all that has happened is that the scratches have been polished leaving an uneven surface to the metal. In an attempt to get a good reflective finish, the polisher has started to round the edges.

A component being cleaned up on some carat paper. The carat paper has been fixed to a sheet of plate glass using double-sided tape so that it is perfectly flat.

To achieve the finest results you should start with the coarsest grade of emery paper. Move the piece of work carefully up and down in one direction until all the scratches are running the same way. Move down one grade of paper, but this time move your work across the emery paper so that the scratches run across those scratches previously made. This method makes it easy to tell when you have removed the scratches made by the coarser paper. If a deeper scratch is visible at this stage, you must go back to the coarse paper and start again. This process should then be repeated using all the remaining grades of paper. If a deeper scratch is made accidentally when using one of the finer grades, it may only be necessary to repolish with the previous grade so that not too much metal is removed.

If you have carried out the work correctly, the edges should remain sharp and only a minimal amount of finishing should be necessary, either with the polishing motor or by hand. If your work is to have a satin emery polish (straight grained), use a fresh part of the paper for the final pass, or you may end up with an uneven finish if the paper is clogged up.

The grit on the paper will lose some of its abrasiveness with use and will become finer. This paper can then be used as a finer grade paper on work that does not have a highly polished large surface area.

Emery paper can also be used with the pendant motor. You will need to cut the mop off an old pendant mop motor and then cut a slot down the centre of the shaft with a piercing saw. One end of a strip of emery can be fitted into the slot while the remainder of the strip is wrapped around the shaft in the same direction as that in which the motor turns.

Wet-and-Dry Paper

This an alternative form of abrasive paper and can be used either wet or dry. Better results are achieved if it is used wet, as the water will help prevent the metal clogging in the grit.

Carat Paper

Carat paper was developed for polishing platinum, which clogs other papers. It is used dry, and a good tap will remove most of the metal when it becomes clogged.

Natural Stone

Natural stone can also be used to finish work, and leaves a fine surface comparable to 4/0 or 3/0 emery paper. The stone which is most commonly used is Water of

Ayr stone (a form of slate). In jewellery making this stone is used to remove fire-stain. Water is used which acts as a lubricant, leaving a finer finish. However, it is a messy process, with the stone being worn away until it becomes a mud which must be removed. Water of Ayr stone will give a good matt finish and gives silver a pale green tint.

Another stone that is used is Arkansas stone. It is used for the final sharpening of steel tools such as gravers and scorpers. It is used with oil, and a fine stone will leave a polished finish. Arkansan stones are very fragile, so care must be taken not to drop them.

Carborundum

This is silicon carbide, and wheels and cones impregnated with carborundum can be attached to a pendant motor. They are very abrasive and will remove deep scratches easily and quickly. Be careful not to remove too much metal, as it is easy to end up with a piece that is thinner than you wanted or even to make a hole in the metal. Goggles and a face-mask should always be worn when you are using these wheels as the flexible shaft is held in such a way that bits of wheel and metal dust will fly in your face – not a very pleasant experience.

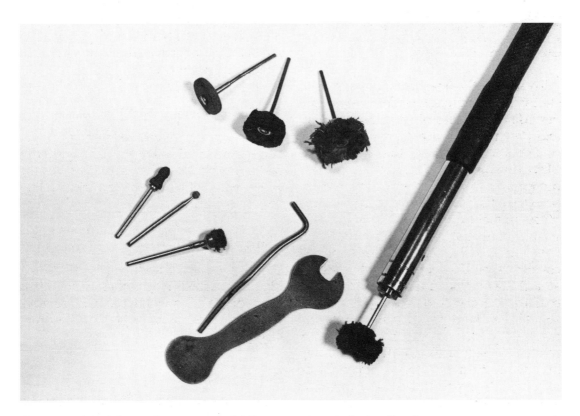

The chuck end of the pendant motor, and following on in a clockwise direction: a chuck spanner; wire to stop the shaft turning when using the chuck spanner; a wire brush; a burr; two carborundum wheels; and two polishing mops.

51

Using the polishing motor. A face-mask should be worn as well as goggles.
Usually you would stand in front of the work which is being polished.

POLISHING MOTORS

When you have used all the grades of emery paper and any scratches remaining on the work are those from the last grade of emery paper, the work is ready for the final polishing. You can either use the polishing motor, the pendant motor or both depending on the size and shape of the work, but most work is done with the polishing motor.

The polishing motor is an electric motor with two metal spindles protruding from each side. These spindles have threaded tapers on their ends and these are threaded in the same direction as that in which the motor turns. This means that the mops can be placed on the ends of the spindles when the motor is running. The mop will move up the spindle until it is tight. There are guards behind and over the top to catch any work that is snatched, and these will also collect most of the dust and dirt from the mops.

Caution: long hair should be tied back and ties, scarves and loose clothing should not be worn as if they catch on the spindle they, just like the mop heads, will wrap round until tight and will drag you with them. I would also advise wearing goggles to protect your eyes against bits

52

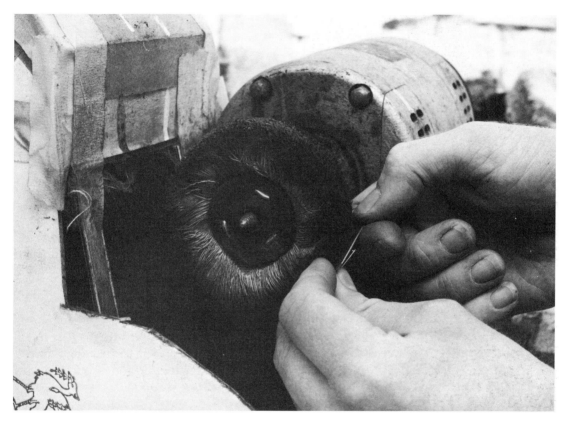

A side view of the polisher showing a swansdown tripoli mop and how to hold
a flat piece of work to the mop.

of polish that are thrown up. I find a face-mask is necessary as there is still consider-able dust in spite of the guards. A mask would not, however, be necessary if you are using a polishing motor that has a built in vacuum or extractor fan.

Another type of polisher that you may come across is a tumble or barrel polisher. It consists of a round barrel with a sealed lid which rests on two round rollers, one of which is turned by a motor. The barrel contains highly polished shot of various shapes, to which is added some cleaning compound and water. Tumble polishers are excellent for polishing small items such as ear-rings and castings and any

pieces where it is difficult to obtain an even, overall polish with the mops.

Polishing with Mops

The mops are made up of either chamois leather, cloth or felt and wool. They are held in place between two leather wash-ers by three flat-headed nails which are fixed through the washers and bent over to one side. This helps to distinguish one side of the mop from the other so that they are always put on the spindle the same way round. Separate mops should be used for tripoli and for rouge polishing compounds (*see* page 17), and should be kept in different containers. Always use tripoli on one side of the machine and rouge on the other as a good shine will not be achieved if tripoli polish is used on a rouge mop.

The coarser calico mops are usually used with tripoli. Felt mops are used to polish large flat areas, but are also useful in odd areas which are hard to get at as, being compact and fibrous, the felt is easily shaped with a file or coarse emery. Felt and chamois mops are used with both tripoli and rouge. The chamois mop is used before any of the softer mops and these are used with rouge.

When you first start using a polisher, I suggest that you use a calico mop with tripoli and a swansdown (which is made of soft cotton) or a lamb's-wool mop with rouge. With the lamb's-wool mop very little, if any, rouge will be needed. You will need 10cm and 15cm diameter mops. Bristle brushes can also be used with tripoli and rouge, and these are useful for those areas where pieces of metal overlap.

Dressing the Mops

New cloth mops must be dressed to remove any threads that are loose or too long as these could mark the surface of the metal. To do this, the mop is placed on the spindle and the motor switched on. The end of a file or wire brush is then held in the mop, and this will force out any loose or long threads. When these have been removed, the mop will still be ragged and these ragged ends must be burnt off with a lighter or spirit lamp until the surface of the mop is completely level with no long threads visible. The mop is now ready to use.

Polishing Compounds

Tripoli and rouge are the main polishing compounds. Rouge is a form of iron oxide and is available either as a fine powder or, more usually, as a wax block which is often known as soap. The polishing compound is applied by pushing it against the revolving mop until the mop surface is evenly covered.

Green rouge is used for white gold and platinum as they have a tendency to drag or catch in the mop, and this type of polish leaves a brighter finish.

Steel can also be polished with oilstone dust and diamondtine (aluminium oxide), using either cast-iron, bell-metal or wooden laps. The laps hold the oilstone dust and diamondtine when these have been mixed with a clock oil or other fine oil. The lap is pushed back and forth across the component with a circular motion. It is a slow and repetitive process at first, but with practice you can speed the work up. This process is mainly used by watch- and clock-makers but can be useful for jewellers.

Using the Polishing Motor

When using the polishing motor, the work should be held securely with both hands and pushed against the mop firmly but not with too much force. Keep the work moving all the time so that no hollows or flat areas are formed and an even polish is obtained. The ideal position on the mop for polishing is the centre front just below the spindle. If the work is held too low down it is likely to be snatched from your hand, at best ending up in the guard, but more likely being flung around the room and causing considerable damage on the way. However, this is more

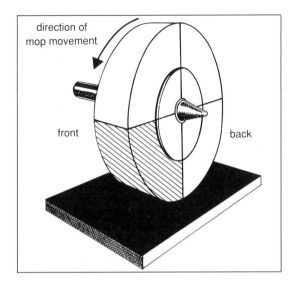

The front bottom quarter of the mop which is used when polishing. If the work is snatched it will be thrown to the back of the polisher away from you.

likely when using the pendant motor. If the work is held too high it will judder and the finish will be spoilt. If the top centre is used and the work is snatched from your hand your face will be in the direct line of fire.

Most items can be polished with the mops, but you may find that some cast work will be too textured to polish with this method without rounding the texture, and a different method will have to be used instead. Chains are also difficult to polish with mops as they are easily snatched and could wrap round the spindles. However, this can be overcome by holding a portion of the chain over a wooden block or an old file handle. The chain must be held tightly over the wood and this will support the chain and prevent it from being snatched. If a piece is snatched from your hand and lands in the

A chain being polished– it is held firmly round a wooden handle to prevent it from being snatched.

back of the guard, the motor must be switched off before you retrieve it.

I find that rubbing the work over with a paraffin-soaked rag before polishing will give a better finish, as the paraffin will prevent the polish from sticking to the work. The mops should be replenished with polish, but not overloaded. Friction will cause the mops to heat up and rouge polish will become liquid, thus giving a better finish to the work.

There are some places that the mops cannot reach but which are still visible, such as the inside of small holes and claw settings. These can be polished using polishing thread rubbed with rouge – rub up and down the threads.

If you decide to hand polish work after using emery paper, a suede-covered buff stick takes the place of the mops and, like the mops, must only be used with either tripoli or rouge. Rub polish on the buff stick and then move it back and forth across the work, taking care not to round off any corners or edges.

An ultrasonic cleaning tank. This cleans the work by ultrasonic vibrations.

CLEANING THE WORK

When the work has been polished it must be cleaned to remove any residual polish. The piece will also need to be cleaned after you have polished it with tripoli and before you polish it with rouge. Clean the polish off with washing-up liquid or similar detergent, or with methylated spirit. Finally, rinse the work and dry it with a water-absorbent paper. Alternatively, it can be placed in sawdust in a drying chamber. I usually give the work a rub over with proprietary polish and a final buff with kitchen roll. An old toothbrush is useful to remove polish from awkward corners and recesses.

If your workshop has an ultrasonic cleaner, you can clean your work in this instead. It consists of a bath which is filled with a cleaning fluid, usually ammonia based. Ultrasonic vibrations then clean the work. This is also an excellent method for testing the security of stone settings as loose stones will be dislodged.

6　Making a Ring

A plain band ring is the ideal starting point for a beginner. The project demonstrates the main techniques of filing, sawing, soldering, emerying and polishing, and the ring is small enough to discard without wasting too much metal if things should go wrong. The complete project should not take too long to complete, so even if disaster strikes towards the finish it will not be too depressing to start all over again. Remember that you learn by your mistakes.

When the ring is completed to your satisfaction, why not make two more rings, one a size larger and one a size smaller than the ring you have just completed? Then you could try altering the size of these two rings so that all three are the same size. If you are still looking for a further challenge, but do not feel ready to move on to the main projects or findings, I suggest you make some Russian rings. A Russian ring consists of three or more rings that are soldered so that when a ring is added, it interlocks with the others. In other words, the second ring added will interlock with the first, and the third ring will interlock with both the first and second rings. This is excellent practice for soldering a number of joints in close proximity but at different stages, and with the same hardness of solder. It is essential to make sure that joints that have already been soldered do not form additional joints to other components or become unsoldered, and to be careful not to melt parts of the other components as well.

Ring shanks can also be textured or made from wire that is left plain or twisted. You can acquire numerous forms of twisted wire. This is achieved by using different shaped pieces of wire, or by using a combination of twisted wires that are soldered or twisted together. The length of the twist can be varied as can the direction of the twist.

MARKING OUT THE RING

Select a sheet of metal 0.8mm thick (the standard thickness for rings), or roll a

A finished plain band ring showing the join as a thin straight line. This would not normally be visible because of the highly polished finish, but has been allowed to tarnish for this photograph.

thicker sheet down to this size. The ring should be marked out from a square corner to save wasting metal. If there is not already a square corner, place a square against a straight edge and mark a line up the side of the metal where you want the corner. You should then use a flat file to file to this line in order to form the square corner.

Set a pair of dividers to the width that is required, say 5mm. Place one point of the dividers alongside the edge of the sheet of metal and the other point on the metal. Draw the dividers from one end of the metal to the other. This will accurately mark out the required width for the ring.

Measure the finger for which the ring is to be made, using the ring sizes. The ring size is placed over the finger and should just fit over the knuckle comfortably without being too loose. Both the ring sizes and the ring size stick are graduated alphabetically, with A being the smallest size and Z the largest.

To obtain the correct length of metal for your ring, wrap some binding wire around the appropriate ring size on the ring stick or ring size mandrel. If you do not have a ring size stick, place the ring sizes on a ring mandrel and wrap binding wire round at this point. Twist the ends of wire together until they break off and then slide the binding wire off the ring size mandrel and straighten it out. Place this wire alongside a ruler or vernier gauge to ascertain its length, and then add on the thickness of the metal. The total will give the length of metal required for the ring.

Use a scriber to mark off the length of the ring against the filed side of the metal using a ruler or vernier, and use a square to mark across both ends to the width line.

You now have a rectangle marked out on the sheet of metal.

Note: when marking out the metal, mark it out on the left-hand side if you are left-handed and on the right if you are right-handed. This will make it easier when you saw it as you will have a larger area to hold.

SAWING OUT

The ring is now ready to cut out. Place the sheet of metal on the bench peg with the strip that is marked out for the ring over the V cut in the centre of the bench peg. Hold the metal down firmly on to the peg, next to the marked out strip. Holding the piercing saw in a vertical position, firmly but relaxed, bring the saw down at a slight angle to start the cut into the metal. Once the cut has started, the saw is brought back to the vertical again. By holding the saw in a relaxed manner you are less likely to cut at an angle off to one side, or to go off course. The saw is pulled gently but firmly down as the blade cuts on the downward stroke on the outside of the marked line. It is then pushed gently back up through the cut without forcing it.

The longer side is cut first, then the metal is turned while still sawing, and the short side is cut. When sawing a sharp corner, you must keep the saw moving so that it will cut a path for itself round the corner. If you do not keep the saw moving in this way, or hold it at an angle to either side, the blade will break. Alternatively, you can withdraw the saw and cut in again. You have to use this method if you are trying to cut a large sheet of metal as it will not fit through the saw frame.

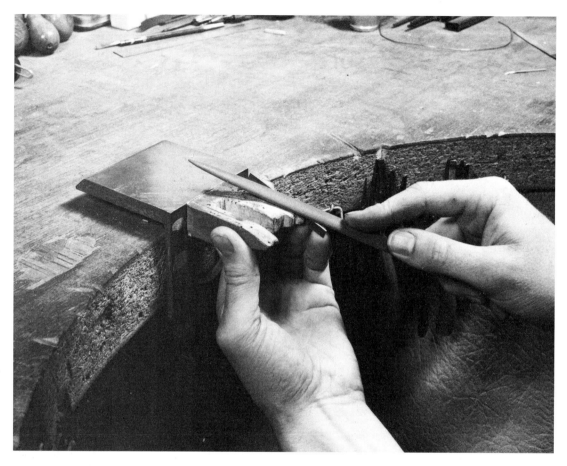

Filing flat the longer sides of the strip that will make the ring. The work is held against the side of the bench peg while filing. The file is held at a slight angle so that a longer pass across the metal can be made by the file.

FILING

It is now necessary to file the two sides you have just cut using the flat side of a half-round file or a flat file. The amount of filing will depend on how straight and how close to the marked line you cut. The short side is easier to file as it is narrower, while the long edge must be filed along its length and is difficult to hold. Hold the metal against the edge of the bench peg. This will feel very awkward until you have had lots of practice.

BENDING THE RING ROUND

With a pair of half-round pliers, bend one end of the strip of metal round to about half-way. Then take the other end and bend it round until both ends meet. With a pair of flat or parallel pliers, flatten both ends where they join. Alternatively, overlap the ends and then cut through the two overlaps to get two parallel ends. To obtain a close fit, overlap the ends until they snap back together snugly. To align the

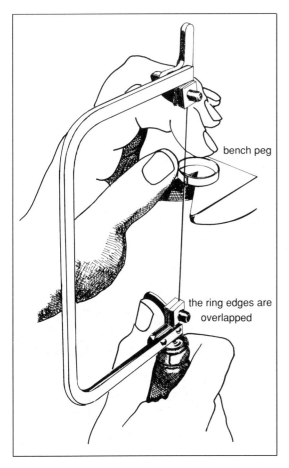

The ring being cut through to form two
straight parallel ends using the piercing saw.

sides, push each side of the join in opposite directions until they also line up. It
is very important that there is no gap between the two edges as the solder will not
fill it.

SOLDERING

Set the ring on its side and, using a fine
brush, paint around the join with borax. If
the ring is silver use argo-tech as well.
Gently heat the join until the water in the
borax (or argo-tech) has boiled off, causing the borax to turn white, bubble up
and drop back on to the join. Using a pair
of tweezers, pick up a paillon of hard solder and dip it into the borax. Do not drop
the paillon into the borax as it will be difficult to retrieve. Place the dipped paillon
over the join. One paillon of solder will be
sufficient to solder the ring, but a second
one can be placed on the join if you have
not had much previous practice in
soldering.

Heat the whole ring up and when it
starts to turn red, move the flame over the
join at an angle so that the back of the ring

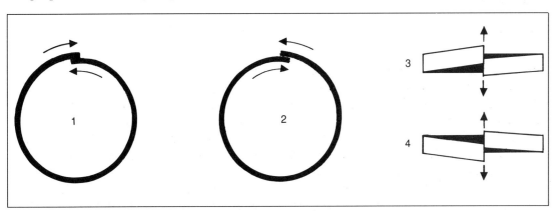

1 and 2 show the ring being overlapped to spring the ends slightly so that they
rest together; 3 and 4 show how to align the sides of the join.

61

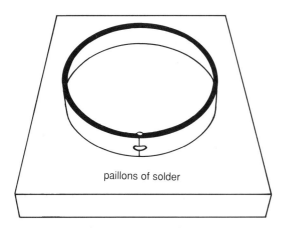

paillons of solder

Placing the ring on the soldering block and placing the paillons of solder over the joint.

is still in contact with the end of the flame. As the ring starts to turn an orange/red colour, the solder will form a ball and will then run as a silver streak down the join. Remove the flame. If the solder forms a ball and does not seem to move then more heat is needed. Let the ring cool down a little and then pick it up with a pair of self-locking tweezers and quench it in water.

Use brass or plastic tweezers to put the ring into the pickle to clean off the borax and oxides. When the ring is clean, take it out of the pickle using tweezers once again. Wash the ring in water and dry thoroughly.

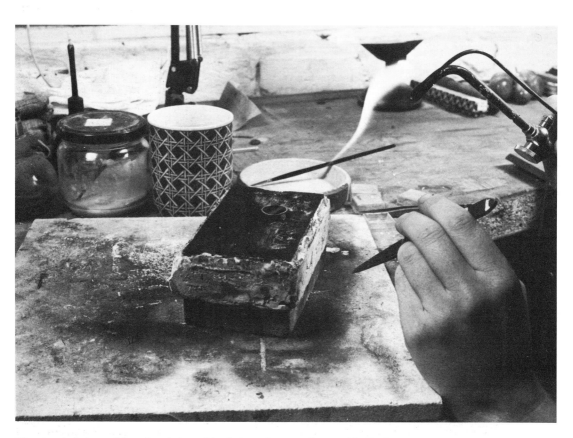

The ring is being soldered and the solder is just about to flow, with the borax on the joint still visible.

ROUNDING THE RING AND FINAL FILING

With the curved edge of a half-round file, use a circular motion across the solder join to file the inside of the join so that any surplus solder is removed. Place the ring on a mandrel or triblet, and hammer round the ring using a rawhide or nylon mallet until the join is reached again. Take the ring off the mandrel, place it the other way up and hammer round again. Repeat this process until the ring is perfectly round.

Check the size on a ring size stick – it should be the right size or slightly larger.

If it is larger, cut through the joint and overlap the edges, then cut through the overlap and resolder. If the ring is too small, place it on the mandrel and hammer it until it is the right size. If the ring is half a size smaller or more, it is advisable to insert an extra piece of metal. This will mean cutting through the ring and opening it so that it can take the piece to be inserted. Then solder it back together.

When the ring is the right size, file the outside surface using a flat file or the flat side of a half-round file. Before filing, the outside edges of the ring will be slightly higher than at the centre. When filing, follow the curve of the ring so that you do not file a flat piece on the surface of the ring.

Rounding the ring on the triblet using the rawhide mallet to tap round it.

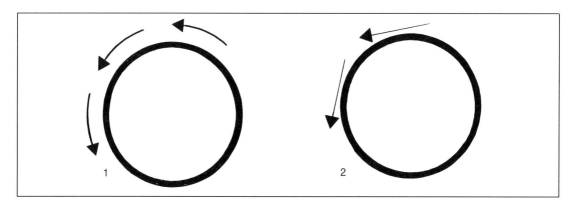

When filing round the outside of the ring, you file following the contour of the curve, as in 1 and not in a series of flats, as in 2.

File around the ring until the edges are level with the centre, and then file a slight bevel on the outside and inside edges to take off the burrs. If you are making a textured ring, you will need to make it slightly smaller than your ring size as the ring will stretch when you hammer on the texture, unless, of course, you are applying the texture by filing.

If you are using silver and have any fire-stain, remove it with Water of Ayr stone. The fire-stain will show up as a purple patch on the surface of the metal; especially when it has been polished. Dip the Water of Ayr stone in water as this will give it some lubrication and leaves a fine finish. Rub the stone over the fire-stain until it has been removed. Small areas can be polished out, but take care not to round off the edges.

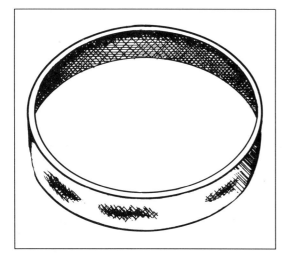

This shows how the fire-stain would appear round the outside of the ring.

POLISHING

Work through the grades of emery paper from 0 to 3/0 in alternate directions. When the scratches that were made by filing have been removed by a coarse grade of emery, another finer grade is used in the opposite direction to remove the scratches made by the coarser grade. By working in a different direction each time, the scratches from the grade previously used will show up, thus making it easy to see when they have been removed.

When you have progressed through all the grades, rub the ring with a paraffin-soaked rag to prevent the polish from

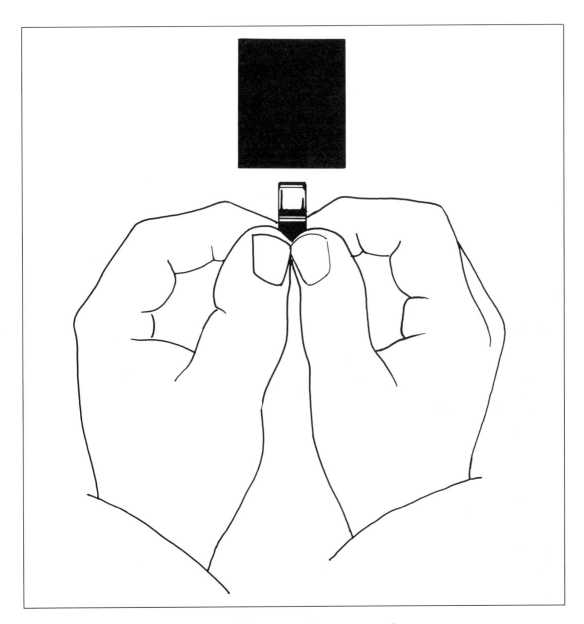

Presenting and holding the ring to the polishing mop. Never put your finger through the ring to hold it.

sticking to the ring. Start your polishing process by applying tripoli to the tripoli mop – to do this, place the block of polish against the mop for a short time.

Hold the ring with both thumbs and first fingers. Place your fingers on the inside of the ring with your thumbs on top. Present the ring to the mop using the lower quarter of the mop. Turn the ring with your thumbs and fingers in opposite

65

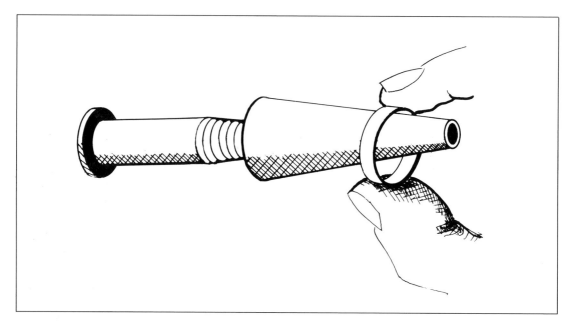

The inside of the ring being polished using a felt cone.

directions until the scratches made by the 3/0 emery paper have been removed. Wipe the ring with paraffin to remove the tripoli, and then wipe on some more paraffin.

Next, repeat the polishing process as before, but use a rouge mop and rouge polish. When the outside of the ring is polished, repeat the process for the inside using a felt polishing cone. To do this, hold the ring on the outside and place it on the cone so that the cone is touching the ring. Then slowly move it around until the inside is polished. If the ring snags or sticks on the cone, turn off the polisher, remove the ring and then start again. Do not try to remove the ring when the polisher is turned on.

When the polishing is complete, either wash the ring with washing-up liquid or rub it around with a proprietary polish to remove any surplus tripoli or rouge. Clean the ring with a clean cloth or piece of kitchen towel. The ring is now finished.

RUSSIAN RINGS

To make a Russian ring with three rings, use half-round wire and make each ring a size larger than required to allow for the interlocking. If more rings are used, make them an extra size larger to allow for the extra metal used. A ring mandrel with a groove cut along its length is also useful to round the rings. Solder round and clean the first ring and then thread a second ring on to the first and solder this. The third ring is threaded on to the first and second rings, and then also soldered. The complete ring is then cleaned and polished as for a normal ring.

7 Findings

Findings cover a wide range of components which are almost complete pieces in themselves. They are the humble fittings and catches for securing pieces of jewellery, and are often taken for granted. They can vary from the crude but effective to the intricate and ornamental, and reflect the piece of work to which they are attached.

A very wide range of mass-produced findings are available, so it is not really necessary to make your own. If, however, you cannot obtain the finding you are looking for, or a mass-produced finding is not suitable for your design, you will need to make your own. Also you will find that a well-executed, handmade finding will greatly enhance and complement your work, whilst a mass-produced finding could detract from the finished piece. The experience gained from making a finding will improve your general technique as the work involved is on a small scale and very exacting. If it is not done correctly, the finding will not function properly. There are obviously many different types of findings, but I will only show you how to make two variations of each category of findings – a simple version and a more elegant version.

Generally speaking, you will obtain a more professional finish if you use mass-produced ear-ring butterflies and wire hooks as you will find it very difficult to produce a perfectly balanced pair unless you make them regularly. I would also advise you to buy any findings that have built-in springs, such as clip-on ear-ring clips, spring-bar cuff-link backs and bolt rings. A bolt ring is a hollow jump ring with an opening and with a wire running inside which is attached to a spring. When a tag is pulled back, the wire is drawn across the opening to allow a jump ring to enter the bolt ring. When the tag is released, the wire springs back across the opening, holding the jump ring in place. Safety chains are also very fiddly for the beginner to make and so should be purchased at this stage.

Every piece of work that you make will require a different sized finding, so you must match your finding as closely as possible to the work. You will then have to make the finding bigger or smaller so that it fits exactly. When designing a piece you must remember that the finding is an integral part of the finished article, and not something that is stuck on as an afterthought.

JUMP RINGS

Jump rings are small, round rings that are used to hold other findings on, and to provide links so that lengths of chain can be made.

When making jump rings, wire is simply wrapped round a former, so the ring can be square, triangular, oval, round or any shape within reason. Any shape of wire can be used.

Anneal the wire and then clamp it

against the former in the vice. Wrap a piece of paper round the former once, and hold it at one end with some tape. Wrap the wire round the former, keeping the coils tight and close against each other, until all the wire is used up. Release the wire and former from the vice, and the rings should slide off. If the rings do not slide off, heat the rings and former to burn away the paper – they should do so now. Once the rings are off, anneal them and then clean them in the pickle before drying them off.

Now comes the hard part – you must cut the rings. Thread the saw blade through the centre of the rings and tighten the saw blade again. Hold the coil of wire on the slope of the bench peg with your thumb and forefinger round the peg. With your other hand, carefully make a straight cut at an angle, so that you then cut several rings out all at the same time.

Now – and here is the clever part – as each ring is cut through it will drop on to the back of the saw blade and slide down it, so that when all the rings have been cut, the saw blade can simply be undone so that the rings slide off into a container positioned below.

To open up the rings, hold each on either side of the join or cut with two flat-nose pliers, and twist in opposite directions so that the ring is kept round. The rings are closed in the same way. When the rings are opened you can file the joint to remove any burrs and to give a clean flat surface for soldering.

If you find it awkward to cut the rings downwards through the centre of the coil, they can be cut from the top. However, they will not collect on the saw blade but will fall into the sling below the work-bench.

EAR-RING FINDINGS

There are several forms of ear-ring fastenings ranging from wire hooks to clips for pierced and non-pierced ears. The two examples given are the most popular for pierced ears.

Wire Hook Ear-Ring

This fastening consists of a simple wire hook. You should use 0.8mm round wire or smaller – 0.8mm is the largest size used for ear-ring wires, with 0.6mm being the ideal size as it is thick enough to have sufficient strength, but fine enough to look elegant.

Start with a length of wire 30–35mm long. File both ends round, and then file a taper on one end, but not to a sharp point. With a pair of round-nose pliers, form a ring on the end opposite the taper. (The finished wire will resemble a shepherd's crook in shape.) Hold the wire at an angle so that it goes up at a slight angle over the ring. With a pair of half-round pliers, start bending the wire over so that it forms a half-round circle about 3 or 4mm from the ring. Bend this circle round slightly more than half-way, so that the tapered end is sloping in towards the ring. Bend the taper out from the ring until it is level with the top half-circle. The tapered part will look more pleasing if it is finished with a gentle curve.

Safety-Wire Hook Ear-Ring

This ear-ring hook is the same as the previous one, but it incorporates a safety hook to prevent it from falling out. The wire used for this hook should be 8–10mm longer than for the wire hook ear-

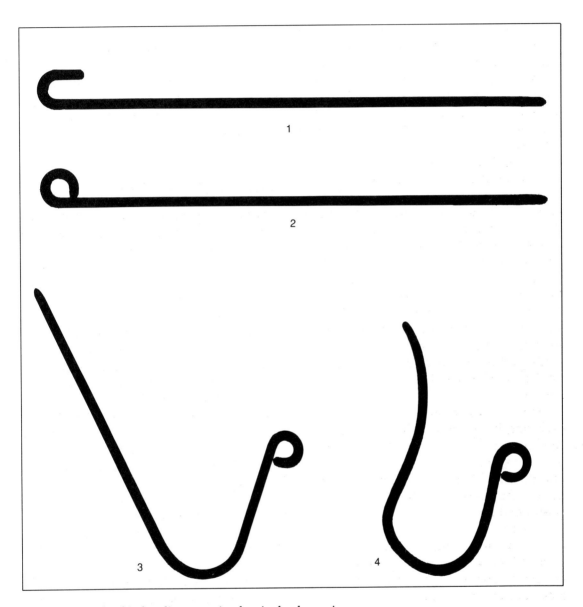

The stages involved in bending up a simple wire hook ear-ring.

ring (40–45mm). Instead of bending a ring on one end, a hook is made that holds satisfactorily the thickness of wire being used.

To make the hook, hold the wire in a pair of flat-nose pliers and bend it down. About 4mm along, making sure that the hook is out to one side at 90° to the wire, form a small ring taking the tapered end of the wire upward. The part of the wire that forms the ring can either be crossed over, or can be kept on the same plane, leaving a gap facing into the centre of the hook.

69

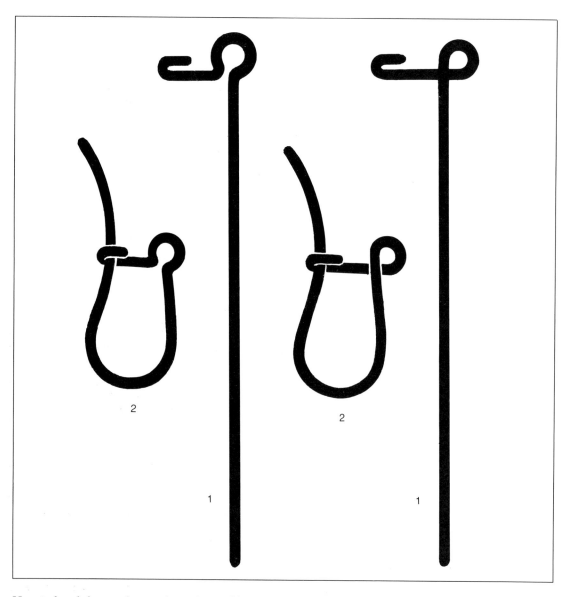

How to bend the two forms of ear-ring and how they look when finished.

Bend the rest of the wire so that the finished shape is arrived at, and so that the back part will fit into the hook. It should be bent so that it rests naturally about 1mm from the hook. This will create some spring, thus allowing the wire to be held in the hook.

Butterfly Fixing

The butterfly fixing is in two parts, the butterfly and the post. The post, as with the hook, can be any thickness from 0.8mm to 0.4mm, and 10–12mm long. One end is rounded and filed with a slight

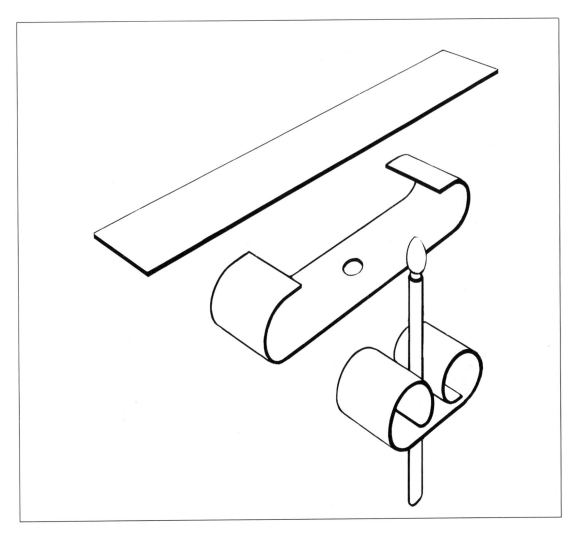

The various stages of making the butterfly fixing and how it fits in conjunction with the post.

taper, and a small notch is filed 3mm in from the taper using a round-needle file. This notch prevents the butterfly from falling off as it catches in the notch, so the ear-ring will not be lost. The posts can be soldered to a ball for a sleeper, to a collet for a stone to make a stud ear-ring, or on to the back of a larger ear-ring.

The butterfly is made from a strip of metal 0.4–0.5mm thick, 3mm wide and 15–20mm long. Drill a hole in the centre of the strip, and then bend both ends round, with a pair of round-nose pliers, in towards the centre, until they meet and touch over the hole. As the post is pushed through the hole, it will push the two scrolled ends out of the way, but these will grip the post because of their springiness.

71

BROOCH PINS

Brooch pin findings consist of three units – the catch, the pin and the joint. Apart from the pin, they vary considerably in design and type depending on the design of the piece to which they are to be fitted. The catch can vary from a simple hook to a safety catch which can also take several forms. There is the same variation in joints – some are like hinges and others are similar to a catch in shape, but hinged.

The pin is fixed on to the back of the brooch between half and two-thirds of the way up, so that the brooch will not be top-heavy and flop forward. The catch is placed on the left, with the opening facing downwards. The joint is fixed on the right.

Simple Catch

The simple catch is made entirely from wire. Start by hammering flat the end of some 0.8mm wire, and then bend it at right angles and file the outside of the bent over end to form a flat foot.

Mark off 8mm from the foot and cut the wire off at this length. Round the end and then bend it into a hook, or a question mark, so that it comes over the foot. The catch is now made.

The joint is made from a length of wire

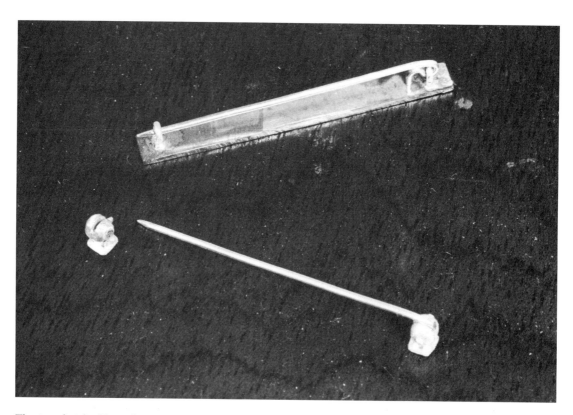

The two finished brooch pins. The one at the back is a simple bent wire catch. The other is a filed joint and safety-catch brooch pin.

The finished wire hook forming the catch.

The wire U that will form the joint for the brooch pin.

that is bent into a U shape that will just allow the 0.8mm wire to pass through.

To make the pins, take a length of 0.8mm wire and file it flat on one end. Bend the wire over at right angles, 1mm from this end, and file the other end so it is slightly flat to form a foot. Make a mark 2mm up from the bend, and hold the wire just above this mark with a pair of round pliers. Keep the foot in line with the pliers and bend the wire over to make a U. Move the outside nose of the pliers down a little and form a ring. To do this, bend the wire round over the top of the pliers until it touches the U above the foot. The remaining wire extends out to form the length of pin that is required.

The foot formed on the base of the pin.

The U formed on the pin that will eventually provide the spring.

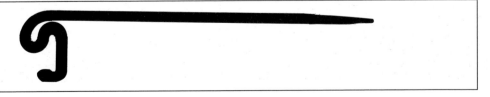

This is how the finished pin should look.

The catch and the U form the joint and are soldered on to the brooch. The pin can then be cut to the required length – remember to add 1mm on to this length so the pin extends beyond the catch. Next file a blunt taper on the end of the pin.

Open the gap between the pin and the U-bend above the foot and insert the pin through the joint the wrong way. Close the gap and turn the pin over. The pin rests on the foot above the catch, so that it must be bent down to fit in the catch when you close it. The pin will then be held firm at its natural point of rest above the catch.

This type of brooch pin is only really suitable for fashion-type jewellery, where a basic pin is all that is required.

Safety Catch

A safety-catch pin is more suitable for quality items, especially if they are made from precious metal.

Start off by making the joint. Take a piece of 3mm or 3.5mm square wire and mark off one end to make a square. Drill a hole through the centre of the square. With a saw, cut down the lines marking the square to the depth of the saw blade. Open out the saw cut first with a triangular needle file and then with a round needle file. Next file a curve on the top of the cut so that the top of the square is rounded, and then file round the corners so that the square is like a ball with flat sides.

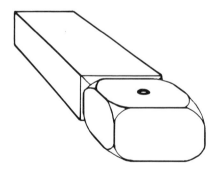

1

A cube is formed on the end of the wire and the centre marked ready for drilling.

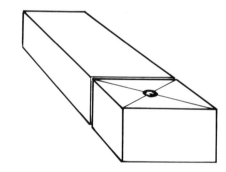

2

The centre has been drilled through with a 0.8mm drill. The lines marking the cube have been cut round to the saw blade depth.

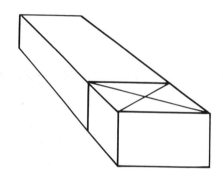

3

Start to file the cube round to form a ball with flat sides.

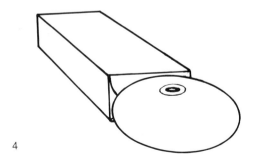

4

The ball has been filed round completely.

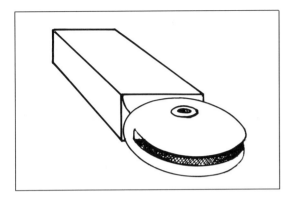

Cut a slot down two-thirds of the depth of the ball.

Carefully cut a slot down the middle that will hold a piece of 0.5mm sheet. The slot should come past the hole, so that it is two-thirds the total height of the original square.

Now make the pin. Solder a rectangle of 0.5mm sheet, slightly larger than the slot, on to the length of wire that is to become the pin. File the end of the rectangle so that the pin is level with the top of the joint, and place it in the slot. Drill down through the rectangle using the hole in the joint as a guide. File the sides of the rectangle to the same size as the joint.

Remove the rectangle from the joint. File the bottom back corner of the rectangle to form a curve so that when it is placed in the joint it will lift up, but the straight front of the rectangle will prevent it from moving down, giving the pin some spring so that it holds in the catch.

The flag on the pin has been filed to the same size as the slot.

A curve has been filed on the bottom back corner of the flag.

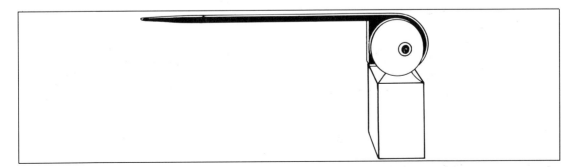

The completed joint and pin before it is cut off the end of the square wire.

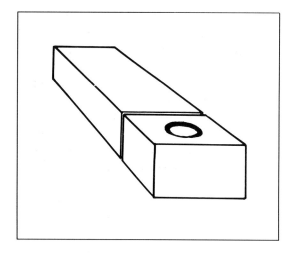

The cube has been marked out for the catch in the same way as for the joint, only a larger hole has been drilled.

Initially the catch is made in the same way as the joint, but a 1.5mm hole is drilled through the centre. When the catch has been filed to shape, insert the saw blade through the hole, and cut down at a slight angle from the bottom of the hole to form the opening for the pin. Do not cut all the way through, and make another cut to the same width as the pin. Cut this out completely and file it up so that the pin moves in and out freely. Make a mark 2mm back from this opening, then cut a slot in the back of the catch, up to the line you have marked. When the saw blade has broken through to the hole in the centre, remove it and remove any burrs in the hole with a round needle file. Pass the saw blade through the opening for the pin and into the slot, and cut down the slot

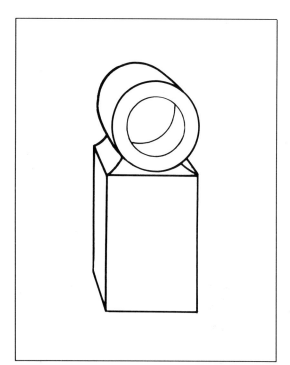

The outside of the catch has been filed to shape.

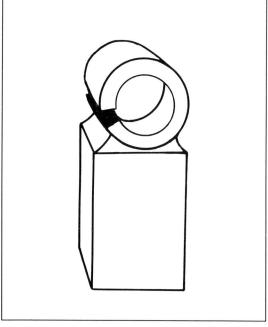

The slot for the pin has been cut through to the hole in the centre near the bottom of the catch.

(being careful not to cut or mark the opening for the pin) until the base of the hole is reached.

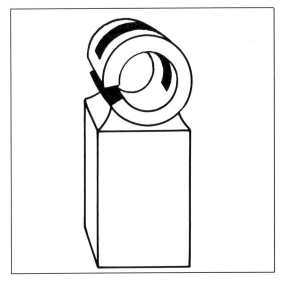

A view from the front of the catch showing the slot cut out for the thumb piece.

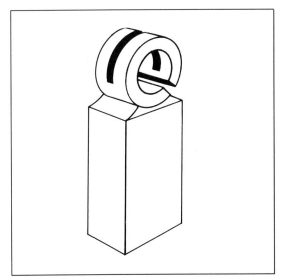

A view from the back of the catch, showing how far back the slot for the thumb piece should be.

Turn the blade round and carefully cut along the slot as far as possible. (The slot should be wide enough to take a 0.5mm sheet.)

Next take some chenier that is 1.5mm thick and that has a 0.25mm wall. Cut a small slot in the chenier that will hold a piece of 0.5mm sheet – this is for a thumb piece. The slot will help to hold the sheet while it is soldered in place. After soldering, file off any excess. Do not make the thumb piece too wide as it could limit the movement of the inner chenier.

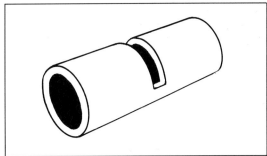

A slot is cut in the middle of some 1.5mm chenier to hold the thumb piece.

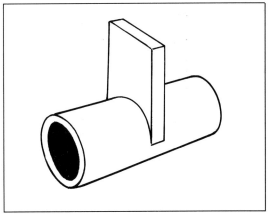

The thumb piece is soldered in place to the chenier.

Carefully open up the front of the catch to allow the chenier into the hole. When it is in place, close it again and move the thumb piece round to the back of the slot. From the opening already made in the outside of the catch for the pin, cut through to the inside of the chenier, so that the pin can go through to the centre. Clean and file the sides of the chenier flush with the sides of the catch.

Next file a notch in the thumb piece. When the thumb piece is pushed forwards, the opening will be closed off by the chenier as it moves round the inside of the catch.

It is advisable to emery the joint and catch carefully and lightly polish with tripoli before they are cut off from the wire. The final polishing is done when the piece is polished with rouge. If they are polished separately initially, there is less

The thumb piece has been moved round to the back of the catch. The slot cut into the catch for the pin has then been cut through the chenier.

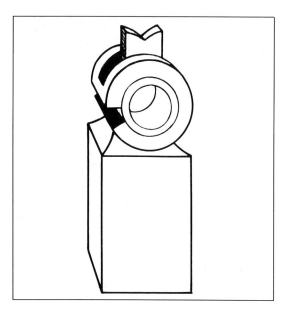

The catch has been carefully opened up and the chenier and thumb piece have been placed in the centre of the catch which has then carefully been closed back up.

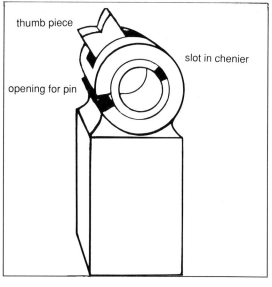

A view of the completed catch with the thumb piece moved round to the front of the slot, showing that the slot in the chenier is now opposite the opening in the catch for the pin. This will prevent the pin from accidentally coming undone.

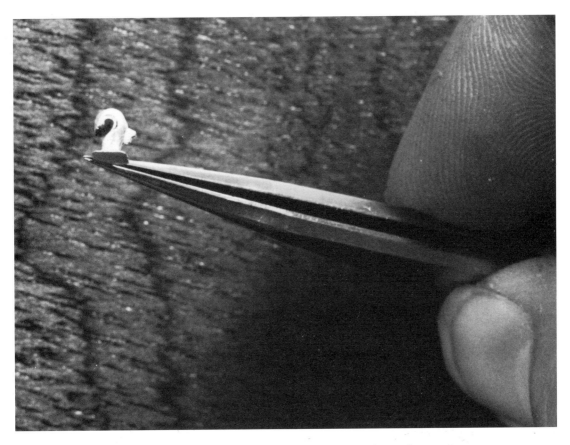

A close-up view of the safety catch. The thumb piece has been moved round to the back so that the catch is open.

chance of them being rounded or damaged by the mops.

After the excess wire is cut off from the catch or joint and the base is filed flat, they are ready to be soldered on to the piece, and the pin riveted in place in the joint.

BARREL AND BOX SNAPS

Snaps are used when a strong and positive catch is needed. This positive action is obtained by using a spring. Of all the findings, box snaps are the ones you are most likely to make as there is only a limited range available commercially. As well as the straightforward box snap that I describe, there are curved varieties. These are constructed in the same way, but two sides are marked out with the required curve. The tongue and spring also need to be curved. Another type of snap has a runner instead of the box. The only difference in the construction of this type is that a length of chenier is filed to form a U-shaped slot, in which the tongue runs. The opening in the key piece is also different as the runner comes through to the front of it.

Barrel Snap

A barrel snap is made with a length of chenier 15mm long with a 3.5mm outside diameter and a wall thickness of 0.5mm.

Solder a flat or domed disc to one end, then file a 0.5mm step across half the other end. Cut a 1mm wide and 2mm deep slot down the centre of the chenier from the top of the step. This slot is for the thumb piece so that the spring can be depressed and the catch can come apart.

Next solder a half-round, slightly larger piece of 0.5mm sheet, and then cut a continuation of the slot through this half-round piece. Solder a jump ring on the blanked-in end and then file the two ends flush with the chenier to complete the barrel part of the snap.

The tongue for the other half is made from a 13mm length of half-round wire that is 2mm wide to allow a gap for the spring. Draw down some nickle or monel to 0.4mm for the spring. This should be 12.5mm long and cut to the width that will fit into the half-open end.

Holding the spring and the tongue, test their fit and then file the flat part of the tongue down a bit at a time, until both fit into the barrel without being sloppy. On one end of the spring solder a rectangle of sheet 2.5mm long, 2mm high and 1mm wide, and protruding over the end of the spring piece by 0.5mm (this will be the thumb piece). File off any excess solder and bend the spring into a curve.

Mark out the inner and outer diameters

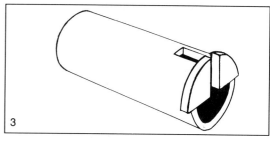

A slot for the thumb piece has been cut through the sheet soldered into the step.

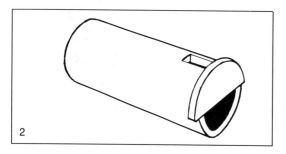

A 0.5mm step has been filed on half the front and the slot for the thumb piece made.

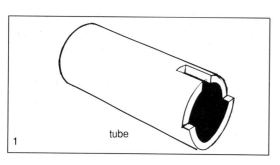

A piece of sheet has been soldered in the step.

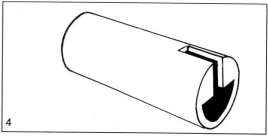

The sheet that has been soldered into the step has been filed flush with the outside of the chenier.

on a piece of 0.8mm sheet as a guide for when you solder on the tongue. Place the tongue on the sheet, lining up the curve on the back of the tongue with the circle marking the inner diameter of the chenier. Solder a jump ring on the other side.

The next step is to solder the spring to the tongue. Place the end which is opposite the thumb piece on to the end of the tongue furthest from the disc and jump ring, so that when the thumb piece is depressed, there is a 0.5mm gap, and just enough clearance between the thumb piece and the end disc.

Hold the end which is to be soldered with binding wire or self-locking tweezers, and tack it together with some easy solder. To do this, place the solder on

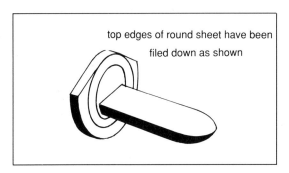

top edges of round sheet have been filed down as shown

The tongue had been soldered in position on some sheet.

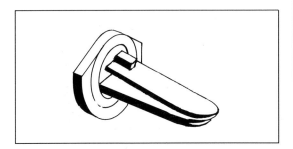

The spring has now been soldered on top of the tongue.

the joint as usual, but heat it until it just melts, but does not run.

Remove the tweezers or binding wire and test the tongue and spring in the barrel. It should close with an audible snap, hence the name. At this stage, however, the spring will have been softened by the soldering, so it may not spring that much, but it should be sufficient to test. The tongue end should fit up close to the barrel with no movement in or out, or from side to side – if there is movement, remove the tongue from the barrel after examining how much play there is. The tacked joint can then be filed off, the spring moved forward or back and then retacked and tested again. If the snap is good, another piece of easy solder is placed on and soldered.

Tap the spring with a hammer and bend it to harden the metal fully, taking care not to break the spring or distort the tongue. File any distortion made to the spring.

When fitted, the snap should now be audible, but if not it can be bent to make a better action. It is now ready to be polished and fitted to the item of jewellery.

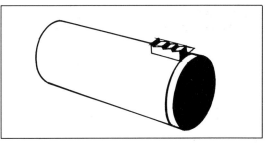

The finished snap in the closed position.

Box Snap

Cut out a strip of 0.5mm sheet, 54mm long and 3mm wide and then file it parallel and square. With a square placed on the long side, mark across the strip 1.5mm in from the end. Mark the line quite deep, but make sure it is accurate. Next mark across 12mm in from the first mark, then mark along 15mm from this line. Make a further mark at 12mm and a final mark at 15mm, leaving 2.5mm on the end.

With a triangular needle file, file across the marks to deepen them and open them out, then use a square needle file to make a V in the metal – not all the way through the metal, but only until a line appears in the metal on the other side. File through the two outside grooves, then bend the strips up at these filed grooves to form right-angled bends in the metal. When all the grooves are bent, a rectangular box is formed.

Twist two lengths of binding wire together, then bend them round in the middle to form a circle. Twist round once to hold it. Make two more circles, one 15mm along one side and another about 12mm along the other side. The wire is then placed round the rectangular box and the ends twisted together. The circles can be twisted to tighten them up to the corner of the box. Putting binding wire round in this way prevents it from biting into the corners of the box.

We are now ready to solder up in the usual way using hard solder. Try to complete the whole snap with hard solder,

The open box snap (before it was cleaned up to be polished) showing the shape of the key piece and the tongue and spring.

The strip that will form the sides of the box snap, with a right-angled groove filed in the strip ready to be bent up.

then if a hinge or other form of joint is added later, easy solder can be used without the snap unsoldering. When you have finished soldering, file the top and bottom edges flush if necessary.

Solder the rectangle on a piece of 0.5mm sheet that is slightly larger than the box sides. When soldered, mark a line 5mm in from one end on both of the longer sides. File the side of the bottom piece of metal flush with the side adjacent to the marked line. On both sides mark two lines 0.7mm on either side of the line that you have already marked. Mark a line across these three lines 1.3mm up from the bottom. Next cut down the centre line to the very bottom of the sides. Lift the saw blade above the line which is

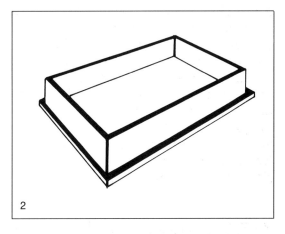

The base has been soldered on to the bottom of the rectangle.

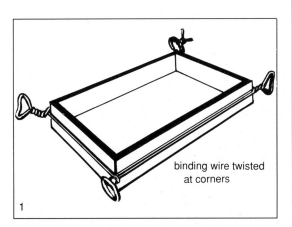

binding wire twisted at corners

1

The strip has been bent round into a rectangle. Binding wire has been wrapped round to hold the ends together and is ready to be soldered.

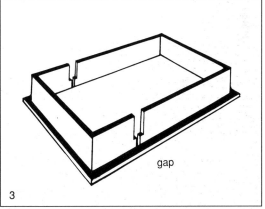

gap

3

This shows the slots cut in either side of the rectangle for the ends of the two parts of the snap to go in, leaving a gap between the two so the bottom can be cut through to part them at a later stage.

The catch in the process of being made with slots cut through two of the sides, as described in the previous drawing.

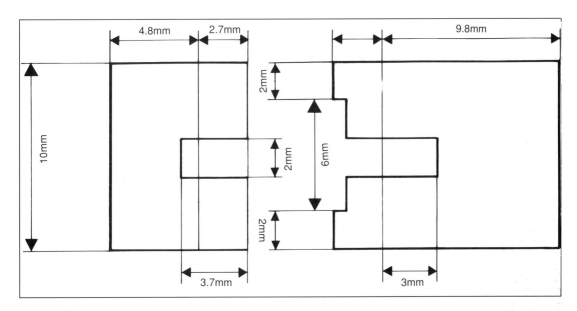

A plan view of the tops and the two ends of the snap, showing the dimensions
to which it is marked out.

going across, and then cut on either side. Stop just before you reach the other lines down the sides, and cut up to leave a rectanglular cut-out. File up the lines.

The next stage is to mark out the two parts for the top:

1.   Using a square corner of 0.5mm sheet, mark off a width of 10mm and a centre line 5mm from the bottom edge with a pair of dividers along a length of 30mm.
2.   Measure in from the bottom edge to 9.8mm, and then a further 2.7mm from this.
3.   Move the mark back 0.6mm to account for the recess for the spring.
4.   Using a square, mark vertical lines up from the three marks just made. Mark off 4.8mm and 2.7mm.
5.   The recess for the spring is only 6mm wide, so make two short marks across the two vertical lines 2mm and 8mm from the bottom.

6.   Two more horizontal lines are then made 1mm either side of the centre line, back from the recess for the spring, in the marked-out area so that they extend 3mm back from the first vertical line you made. Next mark a vertical line across these two horizontal lines. You have now marked out one of the top and end pieces.
7.   To mark out the second top and end piece, move along 1mm from the first top and mark a vertical line. Make two more marks, one 2.7mm along and the other 4.8mm along.
8.   Mark a vertical line from these marks using a square.
9.   Mark this top 1mm either side of the centre line.
10.   Mark a vertical line across these three centre lines, 3.7mm from the line first marked to complete the second top section.

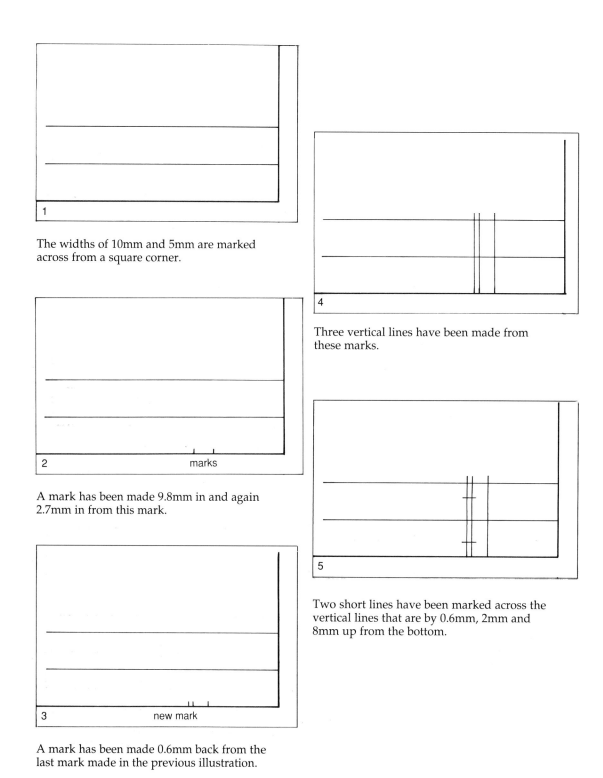

The widths of 10mm and 5mm are marked across from a square corner.

A mark has been made 9.8mm in and again 2.7mm in from this mark.

A mark has been made 0.6mm back from the last mark made in the previous illustration.

Three vertical lines have been made from these marks.

Two short lines have been marked across the vertical lines that are by 0.6mm, 2mm and 8mm up from the bottom.

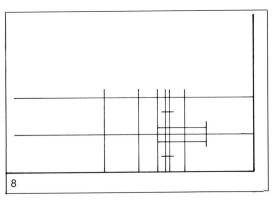

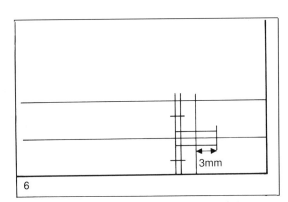

Two vertical lines have then been drawn up
from the marks just previously made.

Two lines have been marked across 1mm
either side of the centre line. These extend
3mm back from the first vertical line. A line
has been drawn vertically across them.

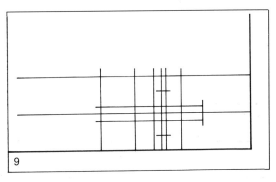

The lines 1mm either side of the centre line
have been extended back to cross the
vertical lines previously made.

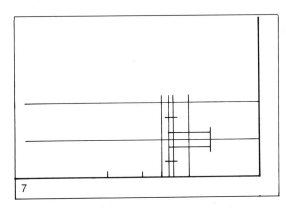

A vertical line has been drawn up 1mm on
from the other three main vertical lines. Two
marks have been made at distances of
2.7mm and 4.8mm.

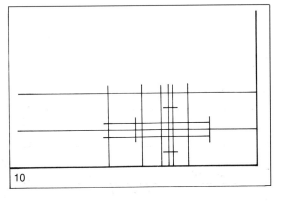

A vertical line is drawn across the two lines
either side of the centre line and 1mm back
from the second to last line you made.

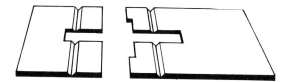

The tops have now been cut out and filed to size. A groove has been filed across so that the ends can be bent up and soldered.

The two tops can now be cut out as shown in the drawings, and filed to size. The V can then be filed so that the end can be bent up and soldered. When soldered, clean the inside of the joints with a square needle file.

The tops are now ready to be soldered to the box. As they are made to exactly the right size, care must be taken to make sure that they are placed correctly on the top of the rectangle and that the slot for the thumb piece is in line. Hold the tops in place with binding wire before soldering. After cleaning in the pickle, try to remove as much of the pickle from the inside of the two boxes as you can. Cut across the bottom of the box to separate the two parts along the gap left, taking care not to go off course. The insides can be dried better now as the openings are more accessible. When dry, file up the larger of the two boxes all round, and then file the exposed ends on the two boxes flat.

Cut out a rectangle 9mm by 11mm from some 0.6mm sheet, and file the sides so it will fit into the lower slot of both boxes. On one of the 9mm sides, mark a line 1mm in from the edge. This piece can now be soldered into the slot on the smaller of the boxes, inserted 1mm in up to the mark made. Once soldered, clean the joints on the top.

The spring is made from 0.4mm nickel or monel, 8.3mm long and 6mm wide. On

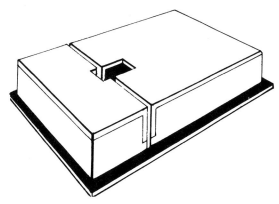

The tops have been aligned in their positions on the rectangle and are ready to be soldered on.

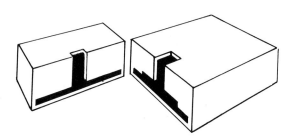

The bottom has been cut through using the gap between the two ends. These two exposed ends have been filed flat.

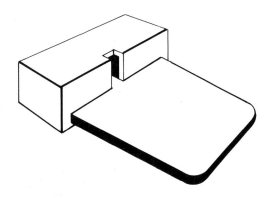

The tongue has been soldered into place on the smaller half of the snap.

A spring has been made 8.3mm by 6mm, and the thumb piece soldered on to it.

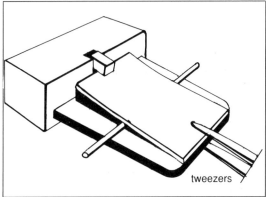

The spring, set up on the tongue, ready for soldering. The end to be soldered is held with tweezers and the middle of the spring is resting on some steel wire, so that the other end will not get soldered accidentally.

tweezers

one of the 6mm ends, solder a thumb piece that is 2mm thick, 4mm long and 3mm high. After soldering the thumb piece, bend the spring into a curve.

The spring is now set up on the tongue to be soldered. Place some steel wire or binding wire under the end of the spring with the thumb piece, and hold the other end in place with a pair of self-locking tweezers. After soldering, the box can be filed and emeried. The two parts will fit together with a distinct snap.

Note: It is probably as well to make the spring slightly long as it is easier to take some metal off than to move the spring forward. If you are going to use a hinge to fasten the snap in place, it is advisable to solder it on before soldering the tongue and spring.

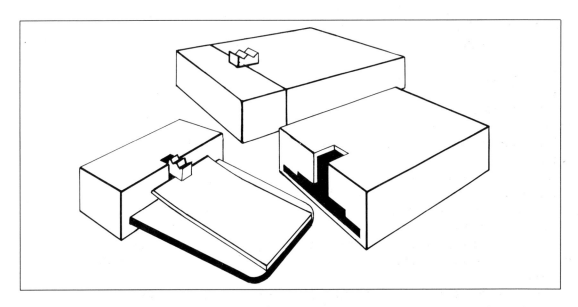

The finished snap in various positions.

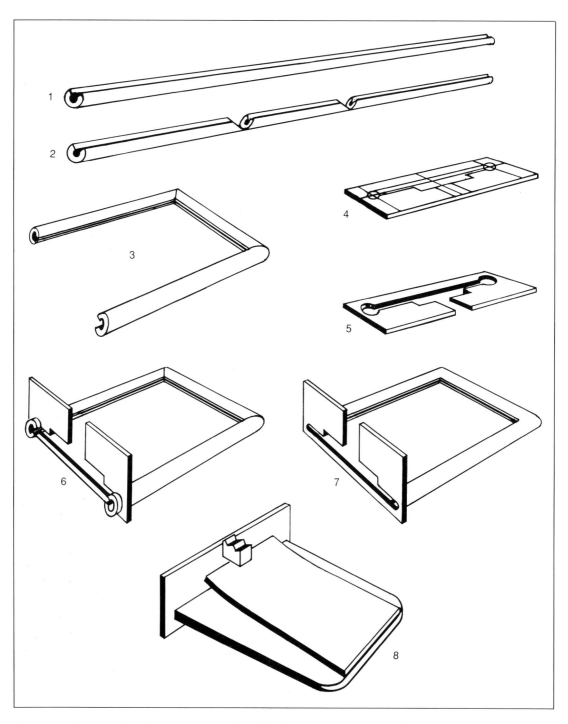

The steps of construction for a runner version of the box snap as mentioned in
the introduction to barrel and box snaps.

HINGES

Although hinges look difficult to make, all they require is the careful preparation of the knuckles (the lengths of chenier that make up the hinge), of the groove that will bear the knuckles, and also when setting up the knuckles for soldering. A gapping or parallel file that corresponds with the diameter of the chenier is used to file the groove that the knuckles sit in. A gapping file is a round parallel file while a parallel file is a flat, smooth file with half-round edges. A round needle file can be used but it is not very satisfactory. The chenier used is called joint chenier. It has thick walls and is seamless, and can either be purchased or home made. However, it is a time-consuming process to make a chenier and more care is needed when soldering it in place, as the joint in the chenier is the part that is soldered to the bearer.

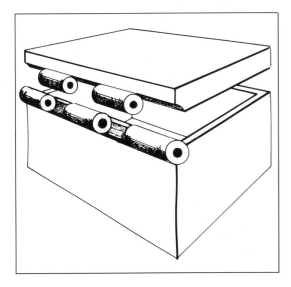

The arrangement of knuckles for a hinge on the back of a box.

Making Chenier

Cut a strip from some sheet of the required wall thickness, about 40mm long and with a blunt point on one end. Anneal the strip and place it in the largest groove of a swage block which has half-round grooves. Place some round steel rod on top of the strip and tap the rod down causing the sides of the strip to bend up. Move down the grooves, annealing the strip occasionally, and using smaller rods until the strip is U-shaped. Tap the sides over to close up the gap until the sheet is virtually round, remove the rod from inside and anneal the strip.

Place the pointed end in a hole in a round-draw plate that is about the size of the strip. You may need to put the point of a knife blade or pen-knife into the strip's slot at the back of the draw plate to keep the joint straight while you pull the strip through the draw plate.

Before the joint becomes invisible, make some cuts across it with a piercing saw at an angle to identify it. Keep pulling the strip through the draw plate until the required size is reached, annealing when necessary. When the chenier is pulled through the draw plate, the metal is not made thinner as with wire, but the hollow centre becomes smaller as it offers least resistance. To overcome this, place some beeswaxed steel wire of the required hole diameter and longer than the tube in the hollow centre. The danger is that the wire will get stuck in the hole. This method is usually more successful if square chenier is needed with a round hole.

Making the Hinge

The hinge shown in the drawing is the same size as the item that is being hinged,

91

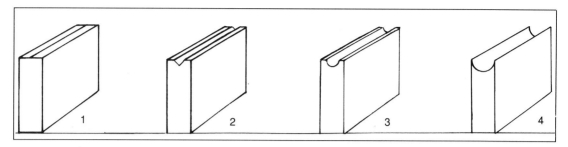

The steps followed when filing a groove in the bearer.

in this case, the panel for a hinged bracelet. This is usually the case for bracelets, but there are exceptions. The reason behind it is that a large proportion of the knuckle is attached to the panel to make a stronger join, but for a box or other hollow item that is to be hinged, the hinge is usually set half-way or more into the box. To make this type of joint strong, extra metal is added in the form of a bearer. This can either be square wire, or flat sheet the thickness of half the height of the hinge when hinging round or oval boxes.

For square boxes, the square bearer wire is soldered flush with the top of the side that is to be hinged in the lid and the bottom of the box. File flat if necessary and file a bevel on the outside top and bottom. Line up the top and bottom and firmly tape them together. The box is now ready to have the groove cut for the knuckles.

The bearers for round and oval boxes are made from sheet that is 0.5mm thicker than half the thickness of the chenier, and can be plain or more ornate. File one side of the bearer to fit the curve of the box. Leave a slight space, then mark the width of the chenier on the bearer and also mark the centre line with a deeper line. Mark a 1mm strip beyond the mark indicating the width of the chenier. Next solder the bearer on to the box, then file the centre

line using a triangular needle file first, and then a gapping file. File the 1mm strip at an angle to allow the lid to be opened a certain amount.

You can make an alternative bearer from a sheet half the thickness of the knuckles which is then filed to fit the curve of the box. Leave a gap and mark on half the depth of the chenier. Cut the bearer out, and then solder it on to the box. The lid and the bottom are then taped together and filed as for a square box.

Filing the groove for the knuckles is a crucial step, as the groove must be the same depth and width, and parallel to the top and bottom of the box, or the side of the bearer. The hinge will not work if the middle of the groove is higher than the end, or if the ends are wider than the middle, as the hinge will slope at an angle, looking odd, and the lid will not open very well. Therefore, the gapping or parallel file must carefully be pushed across the metal with frequent checks, alternating the end from which the groove is cut every so often and holding the box firmly.

When you have made a perfect groove mark this and the adjacent side of the bearer with the width of the knuckles, after you have decided how many you want. There are always an odd number of knuckles, with three being the minimum.

If you have three knuckles, the centre one is usually much bigger than the other two to provide extra strength. This is because the knuckles are fixed alternately – one to the bottom, one to the top and so on for however many are used.

Making the Knuckles

The knuckles are the individual lengths of chenier that form the hinge. For this example, the hinge is 20mm long with five knuckles, each 4mm long.

Place a length of chenier in a pin vice or tube-cutting tool of the required thickness (2mm for this example), just proud of the pin vice jaws and file the end flat and square. Put a drill bit that is slightly bigger than the centre hole in another pin vice and twist it a couple of times – just enough to make a bevel on the outside of the hole. Take off the burrs on the outside edge of the chenier with a flat needle file.

Set a pair of dividers to 4mm, loosen the end of the pin vice holding the chenier, pull out about 6mm and mark round it with the dividers. Cut through the chenier about 0.5mm from the 4mm mark. Repeat this process until you have made the five knuckles.

Remove the chenier from the pin vice and insert the finished end of one of the

The knuckle is held in the lower pin vice while a drill, held in the upper pin vice, is being used to make a bevel on the outside of the hole through the centre.

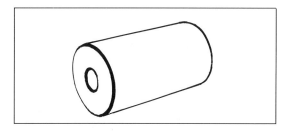

An enlarged knuckle.

knuckles into the pin vice up to the 4mm mark. File this end flat and square as you did for the other end. Repeat with two other knuckles. Two of the ends are left as they are as they will form the ends of the hinge.

Another method for preparing the knuckles is to make a large knuckle which is cut to size to match the length of the hinge. The knuckle lengths are marked off along it. Knuckles that are required for one side are not required for the other so they are filed almost completely away. This leaves a thin strip holding all the knuckles for one side in line. When soldered, the thin strips are filed away. The knuckles for the other side can either be made up separately, or if there are two or more to go on the other side they can be made in the same way.

Soldering the Knuckles

Preparation

Preparation for soldering is the same for all the variations. The knuckles cannot be soldered on one at a time as they need to be perfectly aligned, so instead they are soldered together. However, to avoid a solid hinge, we need a way to prevent the solder from soldering the wrong part. This is overcome by making the area where the solder is not needed 'dirty' –

solder will not run on to a dirty or oxidized area.

The dirt is made from a mixture of rouge and methylated spirit. Rouge powder or rouge scraped off a block of polish is mixed with methylated spirits to a muddy consistency that can just be painted on. This mixture is then painted all round the outside of the groove that the knuckles will rest in, except for the position where the actual knuckle will be fixed to the side of the groove. Leave a 1mm space on the side that is left unpainted, so that the paillons of solder can be placed where the edge of the knuckles and side of the bearer meet. This is to ensure that the rouge does not mix with the borax, resulting in a weak solder joint. The mixture is also painted on the end of the knuckles on the side where they are not to be soldered, and on the inside of the groove where the knuckles do not need to be soldered. Allow this painted area to dry.

Then paint the borax on to the area in the groove which will be soldered, being careful not to allow the borax to run into the rouge mixture.

Now we come to the various methods for soldering the knuckles.

Method 1

Heat a length of steel wire, with a diameter less than the diameter of the hole through the knuckles, in the flame so that it becomes dirty and covered with oxide, or paint with the rouge mixture. Bend the steel wire over to form a narrow U shape, with the parallel sides of the U being the same width as the knuckle wall. Thread the knuckles alternately on either side of the wire U. They should be in line and at the right distance apart, but not in a straight line as in a hinge.

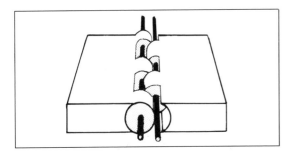

Method 1, showing the placement of
knuckles and the wire on which they have
been threaded.

If the bearers that you are soldering are
flat and of the same thickness as the
knuckles, the offset knuckles can be placed
flat on a charcoal block with the two
bearers placed on either side. If the knuckles are larger than the two bearers that you
are soldering to them, a recess can be made
in the block. Once you are happy with the
set-up of the knuckles, borax the sides of
the bearers where they touch the knuckles
and carefully heat it up to boil off any
water. The solder is then placed in the centre of the knuckle where it touches the side
of the bearers. The knuckles and bearers
can now be soldered together fully, but
only if they have not moved before the
solder ran. If one knuckle moves and cannot be pushed back into place, but the rest
of the knuckles have not been displaced,
just allow the solder to tack them into
place. The misaligned knuckle can be
straightened after it has been cleaned
along with the rest of the bearers, then it
can be set up again and fully soldered. If
more than one knuckle moves, you should
start the whole operation again after any
flamed and surplus solder has been removed. The rouge mixture may need to be
touched up as well.

Method 2

This is more appropriate for hinges that
have an open-backed bearer that does not
restrict the degree of movement of the
hinge.

The two components are set up in their
closed position but with a slight gap between the two. The knuckles are then
placed in their respective positions on
either side. Borax is applied to the knuckles and to the sides of the bearer touching
them. They are then heated up to boil off
the water from the borax. The solder is
then placed in the centre of the knuckles
where they touch the side of the groove.
The work is heated up just enough to tack
the knuckles to the bearer. The two parts
are separated, cleaned in the pickle and
dried.

They are then set up again, but this time
a larger gap is left so that the knuckles are
only just interlocking. Some steel wire,

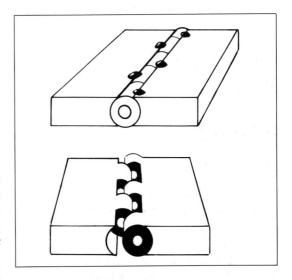

How to place the knuckles for the first part of
this method while they are being tacked, and
how they are moved apart to be fully
soldered.

treated in the same way as for Method 1, but not bent in a U shape is placed through the centre of each separate row of knuckles to help keep them in line. The knuckles are re-boraxed and the water is then boiled off. Another small paillon of solder is placed next to the tacked piece of solder and then fully soldered. The work is then cleaned in pickle.

Method 3

This is for knuckles made by the alternative method. It is used when the bearer has a back which limits the movement of the hinge, as this back limits the area of knuckle visible.

The strip with most knuckles is placed in the groove on one side and is manoeuvred into the correct position, with the strip uppermost so that it is not in contact with any part of the bearer. Apply borax to the joints and heat up to boil off the water; reposition if necessary. Place paillons of solder in the centre of each knuckle where it touches the bearer, and solder fully on. After cleaning in the pickle and drying, file out the thin strips, spacing the knuckles.

The strip with fewer knuckles is then

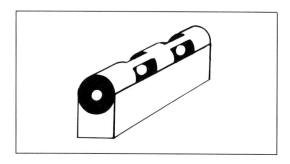

How the strip of knuckles are placed in the groove, so that the connecting strips can easily be filed away.

placed in the groove of the other bearer in the correct position. This strip should be fairly thin and placed so that it is just above the back of the bearer, but not touching it. Borax these knuckles where they touch the bearer, boil off the water and allow to cool.

Make sure that the knuckles are free so that they can be moved for the correct alignment. The first bearer with soldered knuckles is placed carefully on the front of the bearer that you are about to solder, so that both bearers are correctly lined up with each other. The knuckles on the first bearer should just interlock with the other knuckles. Before the solder paillons are placed on, make sure that the thin strip spacing the knuckles is not touching the bearers or any of the previously soldered knuckles. Heat up the piece just enough to help the paillons stick in place, and then place the paillons in the centre of the knuckles where they touch the back of the bearer. The solder paillons are then heated up so that they tack the knuckles to the bearer. Remove the bearer and knuckles that you have already soldered and clean the others in the pickle. The other side can now be fully soldered after you have placed another paillon adjacent to the knuckles and bearers. The strips connecting the knuckles can then be filed away.

This method for preparing the knuckles can be used instead of the previous two methods described for separate knuckles, and is also used for hinged joints on various findings.

Cleaning and Finishing the Hinge

The hinge can now be tried out by passing some wire down the centre of the knuckle

– it should bend back and forth freely. If the hinge is stiff but moves back and forth, any high points or areas that are slightly proud will rub and will show up shiny against the matt pickle finish. The shiny areas can be lightly filed, but first check the groove in between the knuckles for any solder that may have run over into the groove. This will need to be removed with a riffler file or a half-round scorper. If a knuckle is out of line, the hinge must be set up again and that knuckle must be heated up to re-run the solder. The knuckle should then be pushed back into line.

The next step is to file off any excess solder and to fit the hinge together. Broach the hole through its centre to give it a taper and to remove any burrs and irregularities within it. Broaching the hole will also harden and polish the inside of the hole. File steel or nickel wire to a taper and insert it into the hole. It should fit all the way through the hinge and stay in while upside-down without falling out. If more work is to be done on the component before it is polished, remove the pin by pushing it out from the small end of the hinge. Leave the thick end of the pin rather long, so that when the item is finished the pin can be given a tap to drive it into the hinge so that it is held fast. File it up flush with the end of the hinge, or alternatively, rivet the hinge.

CUFF-LINK BACKS

Chain Link Cuff-Link

Cuff-link backs are quite simple to make. The backs are smaller than the cuff-link itself as they have to be threaded through the buttonhole, and are usually rectangular or oval shaped. A simple and effective form of back comprises a plain back and chain. The distance between the cuff-links and the back varies between 10mm and 15mm, the latter being the most common. The links are made to a size that looks right with the cuff-links and back.

Make fifteen slightly oval or round jump rings with a 2mm inside diameter. Take four of the jump rings and solder them closed. Clean them up in the pickle and then thread two on to an open jump ring. Close this jump ring up and then carefully solder it. Do the same with the other two jump rings, and then clean and paint both sets of rings with rouge mixture.

File flat across the top of the join on four of the jump rings, and solder them on to the reverse sides of the cuff-links and cuff-link backs. Cut a slot in some brown paper and place it round the jump ring so that it covers the reverse of the cuff-link, and do the same with the cuff-link back. As the cuff-link is heated up to solder the ring together, the paper will burn away, leaving a very dirty surface that will prevent any of the other jump rings from being accidentally soldered to the cuff-links.

Thread an open jump ring on to the ring you just soldered to the cuff-link, and thread the three links on to it in such a way that they are well away from the join. Carefully solder the linking jump rings closed, and repeat the same process for the back and the other cuff-link.

Clean the backs and cuff-links in the pickle, and file any excess solder from the reverse sides and from the joins in the jump rings being careful that they don't lose their shape. Emery the cuff-links through the grades of emery, and then polish.

This form of cuff-link back is simple

and effective but you must take time when setting up the rings ready for soldering, and use as fine a flame as possible.

Spring-Back Cuff-Link

Another form of cuff-link back is the 'spring back'. This type has the advantage that the spring is easily removed and is fitted after all the other soldering operations have been carried out.

Mark out two rectangles 6mm by 16mm from a 0.8mm sheet, and mark the vertical and horizontal centre lines. In the centre of each rectangle, mark a smaller rectangle 2mm wide by 10mm long. Drill a hole inside the small rectangle, then cut this rectangle out and file it up to the correct size. Cut out the two long rectangles and file them up to size.

Turn the rectangles over and mark a line 1mm in from both short ends. Mark another line at right angles from this line to the corners of the inner rectangle so that you have two squares on either side of the inner rectangle. Then with a square needle file, file at an angle from the edge of the inner rectangle back to the 1mm mark on both the short sides. This will hold the spring. Do not file the angle so that it is square with the top, but instead leave a slight step.

On some 0.5mm sheet, cut out two rectangles 6mm by 16mm. Solder these on to the back of the rectangles already prepared so that the filed angles are covered up. When soldered and cleaned, place the front side up and using a round needle file, file across the 8mm width in the centre so that the 2mm sides have a recess that can contain the chenier for the joints.

Cut a length of chenier 1.5mm in diameter and 8.5mm long, and mark its centre and 2mm either side of this centre line.

Marking the angle to be filed out on the back of the first piece of metal.

The previous step after filing out.

The piece of metal on which the angles have been filed has been placed angle side down, on some 0.5mm sheet and soldered in place.

The two pieces of metal that form the back have been filed flush and two knuckles that have been soldered on are ready to have the strip joining them filed away.

The angle that is filed out to take the spring is in the process of being filed with a square needle file. Also illustrated is how a small piece of work can be held with your fingers in conjunction with the bench peg.

File this area out, but leave a strip of metal to keep the two bits of chenier together and in line. Solder the chenier on with the strip near the top and to one side so that it is easy to file away.

The spring is made from nickle or monel sheet rolled to 0.4mm thick and 2mm wide and approximately 13mm long. File each end on the same side at an angle. Curve the spring and then see if it fits in the inner rectangle. It should come up to the bottom of the hole in the chenier, and press down easily and spring back. If it is too long, file the angle on one

An angle has been filed on either end of the work-hardened metal that will form the spring. It is starting to curve so that it will sit in the slot.

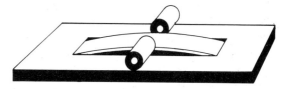

The spring has been fitted into the slot so that it comes up to the bottom of the hole through the knuckles.

99

The back of the cuff-link, showing the spring in place. Do not push down too hard on the centre of the spring when you are pushing it in place, as it will be difficult to take out if it is not the right size – it will then be below the level of the back.

hole through the round chenier. To prevent this, wax some round steel wire that is the same diameter as the hole required, and place it in the hole of the square chenier, before drawing it down to the right size. The steel wire can then be removed and the chenier cut to a 2mm length.

File a groove along the 6mm-wide end of the spacer for the round chenier to run in. The centre 2mm is then filed flat and the square chenier is soldered on and cleaned up. When the spacer has been soldered on to the cuff-link, all that remains is for the spacer and cuff-link back to be riveted together.

It is essential that the square chenier sides and edges remain flat and square – they must not become rounded as the square chenier makes the spring positive, and if the edges were round, the back would flop around.

of its ends in a little and try again until it fits. The back is now finished. Clean up with emery and polish with tripoli.

This just leaves the spacer. The overall depth of the cuff-link is 15mm, so the spacer will measure 15mm minus the depth of the cuff-links, the cuff-link backs and the chenier. Mark the spacer out on some 0.8mm sheet – it should be the same width as the cuff-link back at one end, although the other end can be made wider if you wish. When the spacer has been marked out, it can be cut out and filed up to size.

Draw down some square chenier until it is the same dimension as the round chenier and cut it to a 2mm length. When drawing down the square chenier, make sure that the hole is not smaller than the

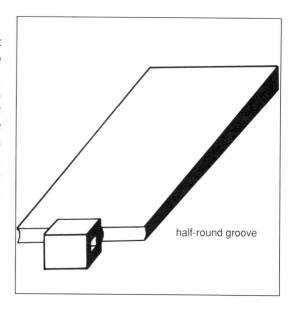

half-round groove

The spacer with the square chenier soldered in place in the centre, with the half-round groove either side.

Excess solder being removed from the side of the spacer next to the square chenier with a barrette needle file.

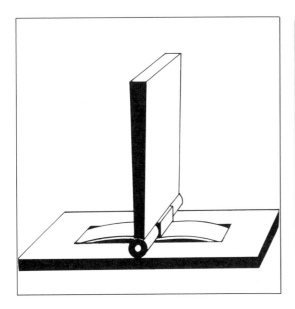

The spacer and cuff-link back assembled with the spacer upright to show how the square chenier will make the spring action positive.

The assembled cuff-link back and spacer. The spacer and back have been riveted together to show how the joint will look when complete, but for a finished item it would be riveted together after the final polishing.

Riveting

Riveting is a straightforward operation, provided the right steps are followed.

Broach out either the hole of the joint or the hinge to make sure the hole through each knuckle is in a straight line. A broacher is a five-sided tapered rod which resembles a small, round needle file and is available in various sizes. It will open out holes, taper them, burnish the sides of the hole and form a bearing surface – this helps the hole to resist wear. If you do not have any broachers or access to some, a drill of the same diameter as the hole will clean out the hole.

Both ends of the hole in the hinge can be opened out with a conical burr or spade drill to allow a larger head on the rivet to be formed. A spade drill can be made from a needle with the eye broken off and the end flattened. Flatten the two wider sides on an oilstone. When flat, stone down the other two sides to form a point. Put a chamfer on opposite sides to form a cutting edge.

Fix a length of wire that is the same diameter as the hole in a pin vice with 10–15mm sticking out from the end. With the tapered end of the riveting hammer, tap the top edge of the wire to make a splayed-out end on the top. Remove the wire from the pin vice and place it in the hole running through the hinge so that the head is as far in as it will go. Cut off the surplus wire at the other end leaving 0.5–1mm proud.

Place the end of the hinge with the head on to a steel block or small anvil. The other end of the wire is tapped with the riveting hammer as before, only a larger head is formed. Turn over and tap the other end again, until the two ends are even and closed against the top of the holes on either end of the hinge. If the wire bends over instead of doming over when tapping, straighten it, file some metal off the end and start again. When the rivet cannot be pushed out of either end, the rivet is completed.

The same process can also be used to join metal together without soldering.

Another form of riveting is to solder some chenier to one of the components to be joined. This component has a hole drilled in it to the same outside diameter as the chenier, and a chamfer is made on one side. The component with the hole in it is placed over the chenier with the chamfer on top. The chenier is then spread over – you will have to make a tool to do this.

To make the spreading tool, take some silver steel rod that will fit in a pin vice and file two flat sides. File down the end leaving a pip in the middle. File a chamfer on one side of the pip and do the same on the opposite side. Harden the steel and temper it to a purple colour. The pip will keep the tool in the centre of the hole. The same can be done with wire which takes the place of the chenier and is tapped over to form the rivet.

STONE SETTINGS

Rubbed-Over Setting

The simple and easy form of stone setting is the rubbed-over setting which is mainly used to hold cabochon cut stones, although brilliant cut stones can also be set this way. For oval stones the ring can be bent from a round shape by bending it out by hand and pushing the stone through the ring. For a square ring, the strip is bent round the stone and is then soldered together after the stone has been removed. For irregular-shaped stones, the same process is followed as for oval stones. However, for ease of explanation, the process for setting a round stone is given.

The outside diameter of the stone is measured by wrapping binding wire round it and marking the wire where it meets. The wire is straightened out and placed against a ruler to find the length of metal required. For silver items, fine silver is used as it is soft – 0.2mm or 0.3mm sheet will do but it is harder to push over.

The height of the stone is measured with a pair of dividers to a point where it starts to curve in. Mark this height off along the side and then the length of the sheet to be used. Cut off the strip and file the ends, then solder the ends together. After cleaning in pickle, dry and place it on the ring mandrel or triblet and tap

round it with a rawhide mallet until it is completely round. Try the stone for fit – it should be tight.

This ring is then soldered on to a flat piece of sheet. Alternatively, a ring can be made from square wire or a strip of sheet that is bent round on its side. This is then soldered to the inside of the first ring. After soldering, the setting is filed up. It is then ready to be soldered to a ring, or to have a brooch pin fitted when the whole piece has been polished. Be careful if fine silver has been used, as it is soft and the metal could be polished away.

Push the stone down into its setting, then with a burnisher, push over a small amount of metal to hold the stone in, creating four equally spaced pips round the stone. Starting with one of the pips, push the metal over at the same time as you pull the burnisher towards you.

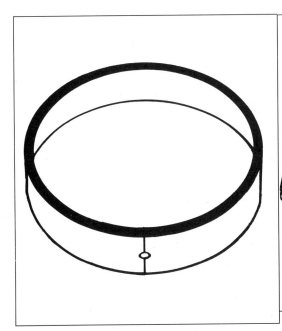

The band forming the bezel is ready to be soldered together.

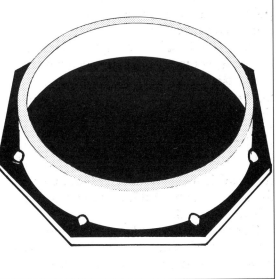

The bezel has been placed on some flat sheet and is being soldered, with the paillons having just been placed on.

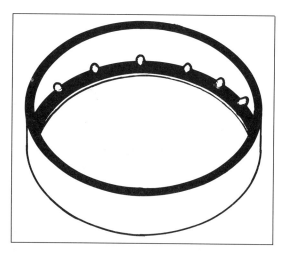

The bezel is being soldered to a ring which will form a bearer for the stone on the inside of the bezel. If you do not want a back to the stone, use this method.

Move the stone round as you go, using the same action as you would for peeling an apple. If the metal is stiff to push over or looks too thick, use a fine file (taking care not to mark the stone) and file round the edges. Go round with the burnisher to push the metal in and to remove the file marks, and polish the metal. The piece is now finished.

Settings for Brilliant Cut Stones

The next two examples are for brilliant cut stones, and use a claw to hold the stone. Although the claw is the main form for holding brilliant cut stones as it allows more light to be reflected through the stone, these stones can also be set with a rubbed-over setting, or held in by tension from a ring of metal. For the latter, a hard metal such as white gold is used.

Bend a length of wire round and overlap it. Place the two ends together and hammer the ring until it is round. Overlap

the ends again on either side and on the top and bottom. Open out the two ends and place the stone in a groove that you have filed in the ends before the ring was bent round. This will prevent the stone from sliding across the face of the ends as they press against it to hold it in.

Crown or Organ Pipe Setting

The first of the two claw settings demonstrated is a crown or organ pipe setting.

Cut a 30mm by 6mm strip of 0.8mm sheet, and with a pair of half-round and flat-nose pliers bend it round on its edge to form a half-circle with an inside diameter of around 30mm. Bend the half-circle round into a cone using a pair of round-nose pliers. The cone should be slightly larger than the width of the stone – for example, if the stone is 4mm wide the outside width for the cone

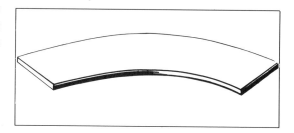

A flat strip of metal whose long edges have been bent to form a semi-circle.

This strip is now bent round to form a cone.

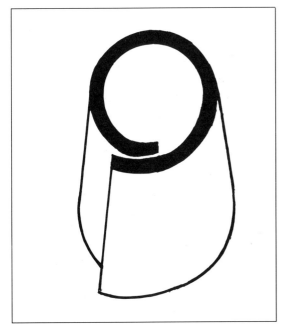

The ends of the cone have been overlapped, and are ready to be cut through and soldered together.

The cone has been made round and conical, and the top and bottom have been filed flat.

should be 5mm. Bend the strip round so that an overlap is formed and cut through the overlap. Align the two ends and solder together.

To make the cone round, place it in a swage block that has conical holes – the cone is placed in the conical hole that is closest to its size. A conical punch is then placed inside the cone, and the cone is tapped until it is round. Alternatively, the cone can be rounded using a small ring mandrel, or with some doming punches placed in the cone and tapped lightly and carefully.

When the cone is round, file the top and bottom flat and straight. Make a mark round the cone 1mm up from the bottom, and cut off above the marked line. File the top of the ring just made until flat, and file a new flat base to the cone.

A ring 1mm high has been cut off the bottom of the cone.

Mark the top of the ring with the number of claws that are required – six in this case, but more can be used as long as they do not look overcrowded. Mark the same number on the bottom. Half-way between the claws, make a mark and cut down with the piercing saw to the depth of the saw blade. Mark off half the height round the outside and also a third up from the bottom and a third down from the top. Holding the top of the cone against the bench peg, cut down with the piercing saw from the cut already made on the outside, so that the saw cuts through at an angle to the half-way mark, but only cutting through a third from the top.

Mark the width that you want the claw to be. File out each space to the same stage before moving on to the next step, as this will help to keep the spaces the same size. With a round needle file, file up the saw cuts at the same angle, until the cuts at the bottom have been replaced by a shallow, round groove. Carry on filing at this angle until you reach the place where the saw cuts cease to pass through the side. When all the gaps have been filed out to this stage, check the spacings and the width of the claws, and use a crossing or oval needle file to round the sides of the claws. It is important that the gaps are evenly spaced and the collet looks round. A pair of old round-nose pliers, that has had its ends especially bent up at right angles is useful for holding the collet at this stage, as if you hold the collet against the peg with too much pressure, the partly formed claw could bend outwards.

Use the same procedure on the bottom of the collet, only this time the cut-outs are under the claws made at the top of the collet, and they are smaller.

Clean all over with emery through all the grades. Solder the bottom of the collet

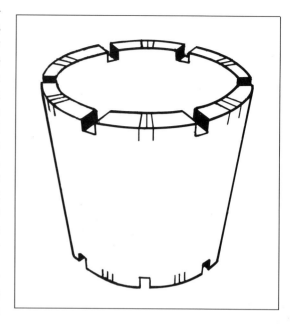

The claws have been marked on the top and bottom edges and a cut has been made to the depth of the saw blade to mark the centre of the spaces.

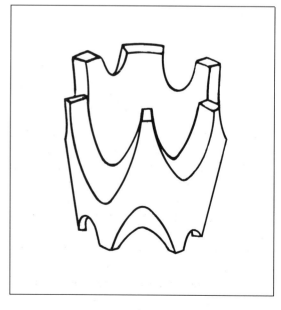

The spaces at various stages of being filed out.

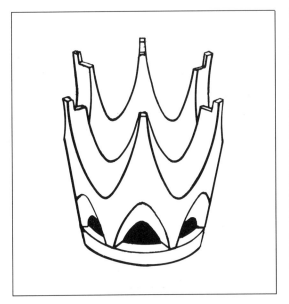

The ring that was cut off earlier has been filed flat and is soldered back on to the bottom of the collet.

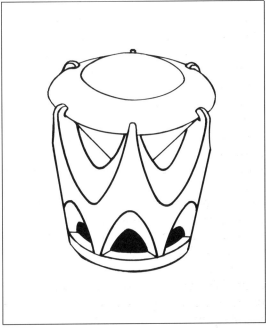

The finished collet with the stone set in place.

back on to the ring that was cut off earlier, and file off any excess solder. Then solder the collet to the ring, brooch, ear-ring stud or whatever.

Measure the shoulder of the stone – this is the flat band running round the stone near the top, between the top and bottom cones of the stone. Add about 0.3–0.4mm on to the height of the shoulder, and mark this depth from the top of the inside of the claws. Just above this mark, cut in to half the depth of the claw with the piercing saw. File away the metal from the cut to the top of the claw to half the thickness of the claw, and then up to the mark with a flat-sided needle file, filing at a slight angle so that the cone on the bottom of the stone has something to sit on. Try the stone to make sure that it fits flat and level in the collet, and correct if necessary.

Polish the piece and set the stone in, first just pushing over every other claw to hold the stone in place. The other claws are then pushed over and down firmly on to the top of the stone, making sure that it remains flat. The claws you pushed over first are then brought down firmly. The top of the claws can then be filed up flat so that they are all the same size and do not cover too much of the stone.

Simple Wire Claw Setting

The second claw setting is made from wire and can be made to fit any shape of stone – round, square, triangular, oval or baguette (rectangular). The oval and baguette stones will probably need more than four claws, usually having two more on each of their long sides.

Cut four 20mm lengths of 0.8mm wire, then solder them together at one end

107

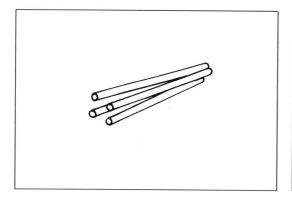

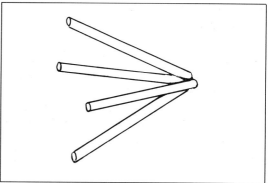

The four lengths of wire that make up the side and claws for this setting are soldered together at one end.

The four wires are opened out so that the smaller of the two rings will fit in near the bottom.

This shows the four wires bent out, as well as the collet with the two rings soldered in place, having had the surplus wire removed.

Make two rings, one to the same outside diameter as the stone, and the other to the inside diameter of the first ring. Open out the four wires so that the small ring will sit evenly in the centre of them. Remove the ring and mark it evenly into four quarters, then do the same for the larger ring. Using the tip of the round needle file, file a half-round recess at the place where the marks are made. Place the small ring back in the centre of the four wires, and when it is sitting centrally you can solder it in place. The largest ring should be placed so that the tip of the bottom cone of the stone is level with the bottom ring when the stone sits on the bigger ring. Mark where the ring comes to on the four wires, and file a small groove in them to hold the ring. Solder the ring in place.

Cut the wires off below the bottom ring and file them flush with it. File a flat on the inside of the wires above the top ring so that the claws, when bent over, sit flat on the stone. Cut the tops off the wires so that they extend 1mm above the stone. Round off the tops and file the out-

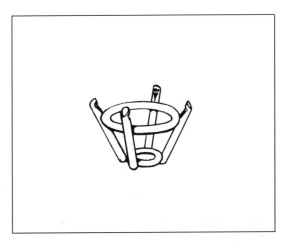

The surplus wire has been removed from the collet and the notches have been filed for the stone to sit in.

side of the wires from the top of the top ring to the end of the wire, filing most off from the ends of the claws.

After cleaning up with emery, the collet is soldered to the piece. After the piece has been polished (taking care not to polish the claws) the stone can be set. Carefully bend the claws over a little, one at a time, bending the opposite claw from the first, to keep the stone flat, until all the claws are flat on the stone and there is no movement in the stone. The setting is now complete.

The main points to remember when making these findings are to take time and care, and not to rush into it. Preparation also plays an important part, especially when you are soldering several items in one go, as with the hinge. Whenever possible, leave most of the filing up of joints until after the last solder joint has been made. A small amount of solder will burn out when the metal is heated up to soldering temperature again, so if excess solder is left on it will not affect the joint.

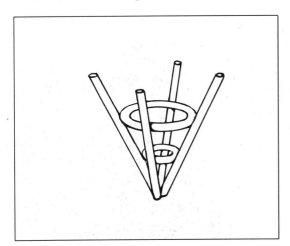

The four wires have been bent out and the two rings are in place ready to be soldered.

8 Surface Decoration

A polished finish is one of the many finishes that can be given to metal, although it is often combined with other finishes. Most of the other finishes consist of marking the surface in one form or another. Metal can be heated so that it almost melts (reticulation); metal can be removed by engraving; the surface of the metal can be imprinted with different textures and patterns using hammers and punches; metal can be removed and replaced in various forms by using a metal of a different colour (inlay); the surface of the metal can be moved to show a design in relief (there are two forms of achieving this depending on the depth of the relief required – chasing and repoussé); the surface of the metal can be eaten away using acids in order to etch out a design; the metal can be removed and filled, part removed and filled or covered with coloured glass (enamelling); and the surface of the metal can be oxidized using different chemicals that will pattern the surface.

Some of these forms of texturing can easily be done by a beginner and in a small, reasonably equipped workshop. Some of them are virtually separate trades, these being engraving, enamelling, and chasing and repoussé. All the processes that I describe, apart from enamelling, can quite easily be attempted on an experimental basis. I do, however, recommend that if you want to pursue them regularly you either attend a college that runs part-time courses or you read up on them from specialized books. They are more practical techniques and are easier to learn first hand.

RETICULATION

To obtain a reticulated surface, start by cleaning a sheet of metal that is larger than the area required. A more pleasing result can be obtained if the area to be reticulated is initially scratch brushed. A scratch brush is a brass wire brush fixed to a motor and lubricated with water. However, if a scratch brush is not available a brass brush could be used instead. The brushing helps the metal to reticulate. Work can also be finished by scratch brushing to give a matt surface.

The metal is placed on a soldering mat or on gauze. Gauze can give an interesting effect if the metal starts to melt through it, but this can be an unreliable process so do not be disappointed if it does not always give the desired results – often the back of the metal which cannot be seen will have a more interersting finish than the front! The metal is heated up to a bright red/orange, and at this point the surface will start to melt. The surface can then be manipulated by swirling it with a pair of steel tweezers or wire. When the reticulation is to your liking, remove the piece from heat before it melts completely. After cleaning, the metal is treated as normal sheet metal using the part with the best texture.

INLAY

Inlay is a subtle and effective form of decoration. The correct method is to cut a channel with undercut sides into the piece of metal. Wire is then hammered into the channel – the hammering will spread the metal into the undercuts and hold the wire secure.

An easier form for large areas is to cut out the parts of the design that are to be of a different type of metal. Then file the edges smooth. The pieces that have been removed are used as a template for the pieces from the second type of metal, but these should be cut slightly oversized. File the pieces and constantly try them in the cut-outs until they fit tightly, having to be pushed in. Any gaps that are filled with solder will show up when the work is finished. The inlays are then soldered and filed flat with any excess solder removed.

A quick way to inlay thin lines is to cut out the line with an engraver and then place paillons of solder on the line. A different coloured solder is then used – 18ct gold solder is effective as it will not oxidize as much as silver or other metals. Interesting oxidized surfaces can be achieved using this form of inlay, but the finished surface must be recessed and protected to some extent from being touched, as the oxide only forms a thin layer on the metal.

HAMMERED TEXTURES

Hammering can offer various forms of patterned textures as well as being used for shaping metal. The metal can be bent to the right or left by hammering out the opposite side or it can be domed using the ball end of a ball-pein hammer, as well as being flattened out. The face of an old hammer can be textured by filing or grinding. When the work is hammered, an impression of the textured head will be left on the metal, and this texture will alter as the hammer blows overlap. A polished finish can be left by using a planishing hammer. Using different parts of a riveting hammer will produce a wide range of patterns.

Many variations of textured patterns can be achieved if punches are used in conjunction with hammers. Punches can easily be purchased and come with different patterned ends. You can also make punches from old nails, or silver steel which can be filed with the required texture and hardened and tempered to a straw to keep the texture shape, as on soft steel the shape would not last as long.

ROLLED TEXTURES

Small rollers can be purchased that fit on to the ends of rolling mills. These have a range of patterns that will make patterned strips. Textures and patterns can be also rolled into the metal by placing paper shapes on the metal and rolling them through the mill. Emery paper can be used for this as long as the grit side is against the metal and none of it is folded back against the roller as it will mark the roller. Steel should not be used for the same reason.

ETCHING

Etching uses acid to eat metal away, forming patterns in relief. The area you do not want to etch is painted over with stop-out and if it is a small piece, the sides and back are also painted with stop-out or covered with masking tape. The acid can only eat away the parts of metal that are not covered with stop-out.

Place the work in the acid and occasionally brush over its surface with a feather to remove any air bubbles. Remove the work from the acid when the required depth is reached, and then rinse it off under a running tap. Additional areas can be etched by removing stop-out while other areas can be covered up. Remember to rinse thoroughly under running water and to use plastic tweezers.

SPECIALIZED PROCESSES

The following processes are more complicated and you would be well advised to have them shown to you in person, but I will cover them in brief to allow you to experiment on similar lines. Of these methods you will find engraving the most useful.

Engraving

Engraving is a process by which metal is cut out from the surface of the work – it can be compared with drawing. Lines can be cut in different widths, depths or shapes to achieve shaded areas. The tools used vary in shape to give different cuts. Usually the graver is square with its end cut to a 45-degree angle so that it is diamond shaped. The two bottom sides of the graver are shaped at a 15-degree angle but with the pressure towards the centre point so that when the graver is held level and looked at from the side, the point is pointing up at a slight angle. This is to give some clearance for your hand. The sharpening process really needs to be

demonstrated in person and practised on some wood first. The graver will be useless if it is not sharp.

A design is initially transferred from paper to metal by tracing the design on to tracing paper. The back of the tracing paper is rubbed over with Plasticine and placed on the area of metal where the design is required. The design is then traced over again. The design where the Plasticine was traced over will have stuck to the metal, and this is then traced over again with a scriber to permanently mark the metal. The design is scratched on the metal and then the graver is pushed in and then along the line to be cut. To turn, turn the block with the metal resting on it while you push the graver.

If you are interested in engraving you should have the procedure personally demonstrated to you. I hope the above gives you some insight into the exciting possibilities it can open up.

Chasing and Repoussé

Chasing and repoussé are similar in that the designs are made in relief. Repoussé means made from the back, and is usually fuller and more three-dimensional than chasing which is worked from the front.

For repoussé the work is set into pitch with the design marked on the back. The outline is marked first, and then the rest of the design is punched out using a variety of domed, polished punches. The work must be removed from the pitch to be annealed when necessary.

Chasing work is done from the front, and the punches used are mainly flat chisel-like punches although domed punches can also be used. Chasing work is also held in pitch if the design permits. The pitch is put into a round, iron bowl and heated up slowly. You must not set it alight as burnt lumps of pitch are useless. When the pitch has melted, the work is placed in it and the pitch is allowed to set. The pitch will act as a flexible support that gives way as the metal is domed in.

Enamelling

Enamelling uses coloured glass that is broken up into small particles. These are placed on the metal and heated up in a kiln until they melt and become one. Enamelling is split into four main forms: champlevé, basse-taille, cloisonné and plique-à-jour.

For champlevé, a recess with a flat base is cut out of the metal and filled with coloured enamel. Basse-taille is recessed, but the base of the recess or depression is textured. The enamels used to cover the depression are transparent enamels. On quite a lot of examples of this form of enamelling, the metal underneath is engine-turned. Cloisonné is recessed and uses thin wire of gold or silver to separate the different coloured areas in the design. Plique-à-jour enamelling resembles stained-glass windows. A design is pierced out and enamel is placed in the small cut-outs.

The glass enamel is ground into small particles with a pestle and mortar, and is then thoroughly rinsed out to remove any impurities. Any excess water is drained off, although the particles should be moist. These particles are then picked up with a quill and placed on the area that is to be covered or filled in. When all the areas are filled with the appropriate colours, the metal and enamel piece are placed on a gauze mat and placed with a fork in a kiln at the correct temperature of about 1,000°C (1,800°F). The enamel is then watched and taken out of the kiln when it has melted together. More enamel is added if it is required and the work is re-fired. When all the firing has been completed, the excess enamel is removed with a carborundum stone. The work is then washed and placed in the kiln to put a glaze on the surface of the enamel – unless you want it to remain matt.

Dry enamels can also be used, and are used in the same way as wet enamel. Enamelling has to be done on a clean surface, so silver and gold are the best metals to use. Copper can be used, but the results may not be as good because it oxidizes easily. Some enamels require an enamel backing to prevent the metal from distorting; this is often made up of surplus enamels. A gum called tragacanth can be mixed with the enamel, especially for pique-à-jour work, and this helps to hold the enamel in the space it is to fill.

9 Projects

With these projects I have included some of the findings already described to illustrate how they are incorporated into the design. When designing any piece of jewellery, all aspects of the work need to be considered: the materials; the type of metal; the number and sort of stones, if any, and whether wood, plastic, paper, ceramics or glass are going to be used. The size of the design also has to be considered – how long, how wide and how deep – as does the type of item – whether it is a ring, brooch, pin, cuff-links, pendant, necklace, bracelet or box. You

Some of the finished projects.

should estimate the cost which will include all the raw materials and overhead costs and the estimated time it will take to complete, if the piece is being made commercially.

With these points in mind, ideas should be put down on paper. When all the possibilities have been considered, the one that appeals the most can be developed further, along with aspects of the other designs, until a satisfactory design is reached. Obviously if the piece is for someone else you would draw several variations of your final design for them to choose from, having already taken into account their preferences.

RING WITH CLAW SETTING

The claw setting should be made first. I have based this example on a 6mm stone, but the measurements will vary according to the size of stone you use. Obviously, with a larger stone the measurements will be larger, and the metal may possibly be thicker, and vice versa.

Mark out a 0.8mm thick strip, 30mm by 6mm, and with a pair of half-round flat-nose pliers, bend it to form a half-circle. After annealing the half-circle, bend it round into a cone. The cone should be slightly larger than the width of the stone, in this case 7mm. An overlap is formed which is then cut through, and the ends are soldered together after they have been aligned.

When the cone has been cleaned off in pickle and dried, it is made round. The top and bottom are filed up true. The cone is marked round 1mm up from the bottom and this is then cut off above the line (this piece will be soldered back on after the rest of the cone has been filed to shape).

Mark the top of the cone with the number of claws that are required, in this case eight. Mark half-way between the claws and carry this line on down the side of the collet. The collet should also be marked into thirds and round the centre. Carefully cut down the marked lines on the side of the collet at an angle, so that the saw passes through the side at the half-way mark, but only cuts into the metal to the mark made a third of the way up from the bottom.

With a half-round needle file, file up the saw cuts at the same angle as they were cut, working all the way round the collet. With a crossing needle file, file round the same area to shape the back of the claws. Repeat the same process for the bottom, but this time the hollows are filed out under the claws. When all the filing is completed, the ring can be soldered back on to the bottom. Clean the collet with emery paper, then measure the diameter of the ring on the bottom of the collet. Next, measure the outside diameter of the ring and make a note of it. Subtract the diameter of the ring round the base of the collet from the last measurement made.

The ring can now be marked out on some 0.8mm sheet, 3mm wide and the length of the ring. Cut out the strip and file up the sides. Mark a line 0.8mm in from the edge down both sides and then a line 5mm in across each end. Each end is now marked into three rectangles – two 0.8mm by 5mm, and the other 1.4mm by 5mm. Cut out the 0.8mm by 5mm rectangle, leaving the 1.4mm by 5mm rectangle in place in the centre, and file the sides flat.

Cut four lengths of 0.8mm wire and file one end of each flat. Bend the wire out at a right angle 1mm up from the filed end. Place one of the lengths of wire on either

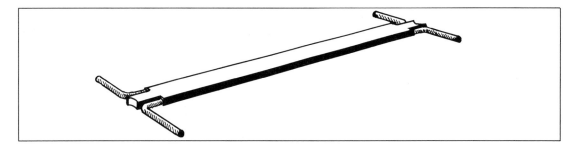

This shows the four wires soldered in place on the ring shank before it is bent round.

side of each end where the 0.8mm strips were cut out, so that the 1mm end just touches the sides of the ring shank. These are now soldered in place and cleaned in the pickle.

Bend the whole strip round, using either the ring mandrel or half-round pliers, so that both ends are touching. Open out the ring so that the two ends can be filed, with a half-round needle file, to a slight arc. Place the collet in between the ends with two opposite claws in line across the centre of the shank, so that the collet is held by the ring on its base. When satisfied with the fit, solder the collet in place.

Bend up the four wires that are soldered to the shank one at a time. Curve these wires in with half-round pliers so that they touch the four claws on either side of the two centre claws. Mark the wires 1mm up from the centre of the collet and then cut off the excess wire above this mark and file the back of the wire at an angle so that it will fit flush against the collet. Now solder the wire on to the collet so that it appears to blend into the claws of the collet. After cleaning in the pickle and drying, emery the ring shank.

If the ring is to be hallmarked, it is usually sent away after the first grade of emery has been used and before polishing, as metal is removed from the piece to

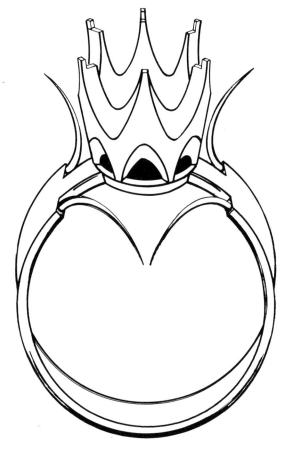

The collet has been soldered in place and the wires have been filed so that they fit against the collet and are ready to be soldered to the collet.

116

test its purity. When it has been marked, the cleaning can be finished and the piece polished.

Polish the ring inside and out, and carefully polish the parts of the collet that are accessible. Polish the parts of the collet that are not accessible with polishing threads – ordinary thread or thin string can be used if you do not have any polishing thread. The thread is rubbed along its length with rouge, and then passed through holes or held against the area, which is rubbed up and down against the thread.

Cut the notch for the stone to sit on and set it in place, making sure it is flush in the setting.

RING WITH A RUBBED-OVER SETTING

This ring can either be used as a finger ring or alternatively it makes an excellent scarf ring. In this example I use a fairly large, square stone.

Measure the size of ring required using the ring size stick and then cut two lengths of 0.8mm round wire to the ring size. Bend these round and solder each one into a ring. Place them over a ring mandrel and hammer them round with a rawhide mallet. Place one ring flat on the soldering block and then rest some steel across it. Place the other ring on top so that the two solder joints of the rings are above each other and touching. Solder the rings together at the joints, clean them in

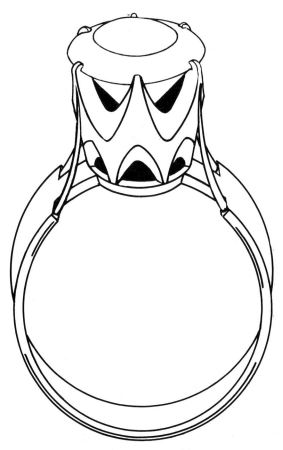

The completed ring. The wires have been soldered in place and the stone has been set.

The finished ring.

117

the pickle and place them back on the soldering block.

Cut off a small strip of wire 8mm in length. Place it on the outside of the two rings over the hollow where they are soldered together, and hold it in place with some binding wire while it is being soldered on. Open the two rings out, at the opposite end to the solder joint, so that they are the same width apart as the stone is wide. Measure round the circumference of the stone to find the length of the metal needed for the bezel. The metal for the bezel is then bent round and soldered together. As a square stone is being used, the bezel should be bent fairly square so that the stone can be pushed through. When the bezel is the same shape as the stone, place it on to some 0.8mm flat

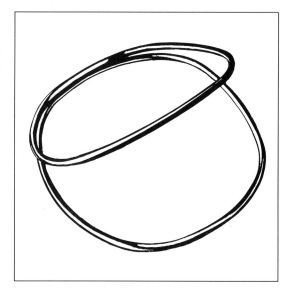

The two rings soldered together at their joints.

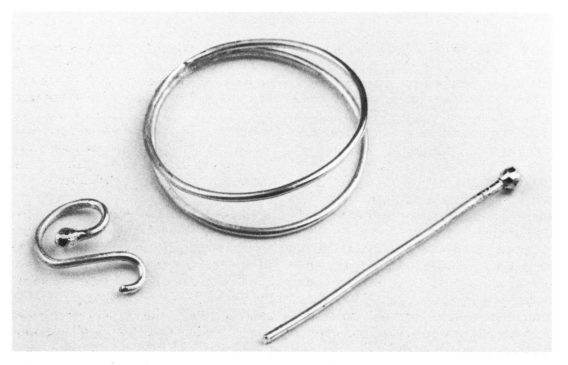

The two rings soldered together, the scroll with the ball on the end and the wire with the ball on the end before being bent up into a scroll.

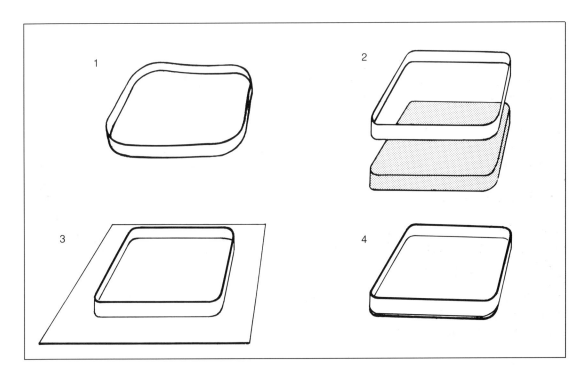

The steps involved in making the bezel for the square stone.

sheet. Mark round slightly outside the bezel and cut this out. Place the bezel back on the sheet and borax both parts, remembering to boil off the excess water. Place the paillons evenly round the bezel and sheet where they join, and solder them together. File up the edges until they are flush with the bezel, then bend the tops of the ring flat, so that the flat piece is the same length as the stone, to make a D shape. Solder this on the back of the bezel for the stone.

Cut two lengths of wire that are 50mm long and dip them into some borax. Hold one in the end of a pair of self-locking tweezers, and hold a soldering torch in your other hand so that the flame is pointing vertically upwards. Hold the wire vertically downwards over the flame. As the wire heats up and starts to melt at the end, the end is drawn up the wire form-

ing a ball. When the ball has formed, quench the wire in the pickle. Repeat this process with the other length of wire so that you end up with two balls. File each ball up and then start to bend the wire round in a circle. When you are opposite the ball, start to bend the wire back away from the ball to form another half-circle as shown in the diagram. Polish these scrolls up.

The scrolls are then soldered in the triangle formed by the two rings and the stone. They are positioned in this triangle so that the balls are facing the same way and the top curve is touching the bezel for the stone. When you have placed the scroll correctly, solder it in place with the help of binding wire. After you have completed the soldering, file the little strip that was soldered over the joint on the bottom so that the ring at the bottom

119

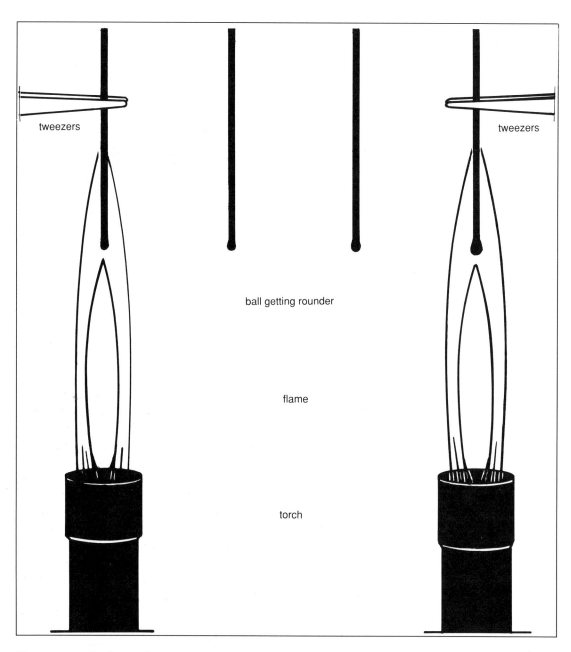

The steps involved in making a ball on the end of the wire.

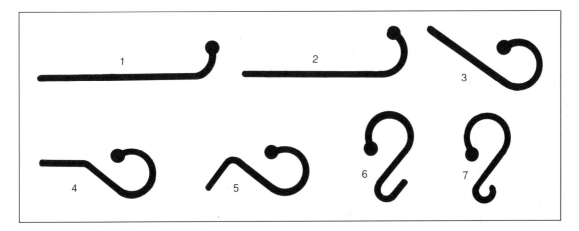

The steps involved in bending the wire round to form the scroll.

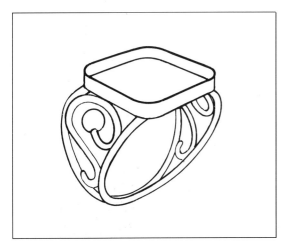

The ring with the scroll soldered in place before it is polished and the stone set.

appears to be one piece of metal. File excess solder from the joints where necessary, and then emery the piece all over and polish it.

The stone can now be set by pushing a small pip over from the bezel with a burnisher, to hold the stone in on each side. Finally, go round with the burnisher to push the rest of the metal over the stone to hold it in.

BROOCH

This uses a rubbed-over stone setting in the design.

As with the previous project, the setting for the stone is made by first measuring round the stone with binding wire and marking the length of it on to some fine silver or on to a thin sheet of base metal. The stone I use is an orange/brown-coloured one and is a flat oval cabochon measuring 16mm by 12mm, with 2mm high sides. As the stone is semi-translucent, it allows a hint of the garment underneath to show through the stone.

The width of the strip is 2.3mm wide. Cut out the strip and solder round after filing. After the ring has been cleaned in the pickle, press the sides so that it is roughly oval. Push the sides over the stone so that the ring fits round the stone well.

Instead of having a solid back, a bearer strip is used, and this is made from 0.5mm square wire. It is made in the same way as the bezel, but is smaller as it is soldered to the inside of the bigger ring.

121

The finished brooch. The different finishes can be seen clearly, as can the position of the brooch pin on the back – especially the catch.

The bezel for the stone. After it has been made, it is ready for the side pieces to be soldered on. Also shown is the stone.

Next, make the surrounds. Mark and cut out the right-hand piece from 8mm sheet, and file it up to size so that it will fit round the side of the setting for the stone. The left-hand side is split into two halves. For the top half, reticulate a piece of metal that is larger than the required area. Heat up the metal until the surface starts to melt, then clean and dry the reticulated piece of metal. Mark out the shape required over an interesting part of the reticulated metal.

The central part of the brooch starts off 10mm longer than the final length as the piece is bent into folds. While bending the metal into folds, it will need to be frequently annealed. To start bending, take a

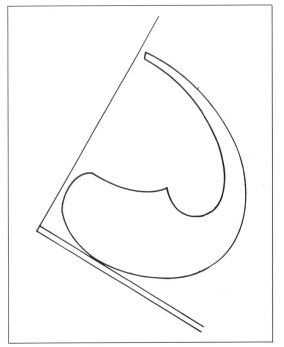

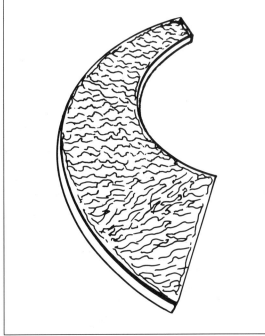

The right-hand part of the brooch marked out on the metal.

The piece of reticulation cut out from an interesting part of the metal.

The piece of reticulated metal, with the part of the brooch that is to be cut out from this metal marked on it. Note that parts of the reticulated sheet have started to melt up towards the centre of the sheet. If the metal was kept at this heat it would have very soon melted into a ball.

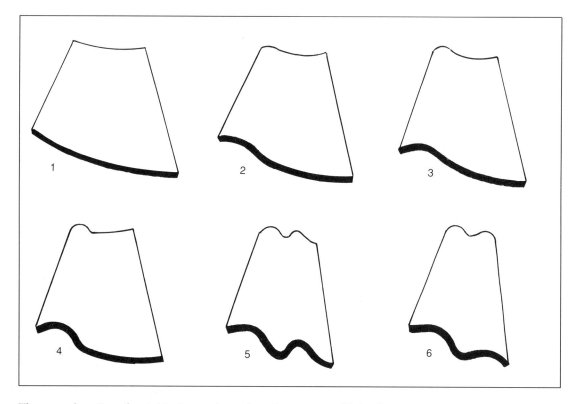

The curved section of metal is shown through various stages of being bent into the folded section.

pair of half-round pliers and bend down one end of the metal. Hold the metal in a pair of stout round-nose pliers and bend it further round to form the first fold. Also hammer the metal round to make sure that the fold is tapered. Move the round-nose pliers along slightly and bend the metal back to form a hollow fold. Again use a hammer to make the fold tapered. The last fold is formed in the same way as the others.

File a curve against the part that will be against the stone so that it fits snugly against the stone. On the back of the reticulated piece, file the end that will be soldered to the folded part at an angle so that it fits snugly against the folded part. Place the folded and reticulated pieces in

position against the bezel for the stone, and mark the position on the folded piece where the folded and reticulated pieces will be soldered together. At the same time, mark their position against the bezel so that when they are soldered to the bezel they will be in the right place.

Keeping the folded piece in position, place the right-hand piece against it and mark where it overlaps the folded piece. Draw a line across the folded piece from the mark and cut off any excess. File the new end smooth.

You can now solder the reticulated and folded pieces together against the mark made. After they have been cleaned in the pickle, turn over and file down any excess metal on the end of the folded piece, until

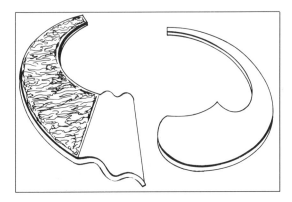

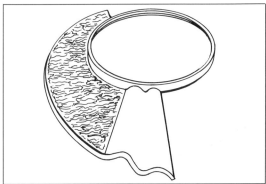

The reticulated and folded sections have been soldered together and filed up to fit round the bezel. Also shown is the right-hand piece that has been cut out and filed to fit the bezel.

The reticulated and folded piece of metal has been soldered to the bezel and is ready for the right-hand piece to be soldered on.

it is flush with the reticulated metal. The outer curves of the two pieces are then filed up to form one smooth curve. Solder the one piece in its correct position against the bezel for the stone. First check that the right-hand piece still fits round the bezel now that the left-hand part has been soldered on, and when you are satisfied with the fit, solder it in place, clean in pickle and dry. File off any excess solder and any sharp corners, and file the base of the bezel flush with the sides if necessary. Clean with emery paper through all the grades.

To make the joint for the brooch pin on the back, take a piece of 3mm square wire. Mark off 3mm down from the end on all the sides so you have marked a cube. Mark diagonally across on two sides to find the centre, and then drill through this with a 0.8mm drill. Just below the line which marks the cube, cut down with a piercing saw to the depth of the blade. Using triangular and round needle files, file this out to form a groove round the sides of the wire. File the top round so that the cube is rounded on its end, with

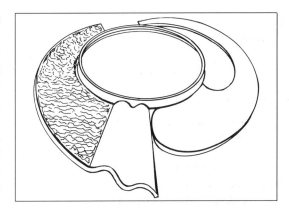

The right-hand piece has been soldered in position against the bezel and the folded part, all that remains to be done is for the brooch pin to be soldered on and the metal polished with the various finishes.

two slightly flat sides. Mark the centre on the top between the two sides that the hole was drilled through. With a piercing saw, cut down two-thirds of the total height of the rounded cube so that some 0.5mm sheet will fit in the slot.

Solder a rectangle of 0.5mm sheet that is slightly larger than the joint when it is in the slot to some 0.8mm wire. File the rectangle to size so that the pin is level

125

Carrying out the stone setting – the final process.

with the top of the joint. File a slight angle on the back of the bottom of the rectangle so the pin slopes up slightly. With the rectangle in place in the joint, drill through it and then file a curve on the back.

The catch initially is made in the same way as the joint, only the hole drilled through is 1.5mm in diameter. Instead of cutting a slot down the centre, cut a slot the width of the pin through from the base of the hole to one side of the supporting post. Make a mark 2mm back from the top of this opening, and cut the slot through the centre into the hole, starting from the 2mm mark round to the other side of the supporting post. Insert the saw blade through the opening for the pin and into the central slot, and carefully open out from the inside to give more movement to the thumb piece.

Solder a small piece of 0.5mm sheet on to some chenier with a diameter of 1.5mm with 0.3mm-thick walls. This small piece of sheet is then filed to the same diameter as the chenier to form the thumb piece. The opening for the pin in the catch is opened up carefully to allow the chenier to pass through it with the thumb piece fitting into the slot. The catch is then closed up. Move the thumb piece round to the back as far as it will go, then cut the slot for the pin through the chenier. File up the inside of the slot and remove any burrs in the chenier.

Before the joint and catch are cut off from the wire they should be emeried and polished. To solder, turn the brooch over, so that the top is away from you. The catch is soldered on to the left with the opening facing you, using easy solder. The joint is soldered on the right, also using easy solder. The pin is then riveted in the joint. Make sure the pin is slightly

more than half-way up to prevent the brooch from flopping forwards.

The brooch is now ready for polishing. Try to get a good emery polish round the edges of the stone setting, and polish by hand if possible as the fine silver is very soft and if you are not careful it will be worn away. The reticulation will only need cleaning with a toothbrush, or a brass brush if there is some stubborn oxide left. It can then be given a light polish with rouge to polish the high points. Only the folds in the centre are given a high polish. The flat piece on the right is straight-grained after all the polishing has been done. It may be better to polish the folds and round the brooch pin with a pendant motor.

When the brooch has been polished and cleaned, the stone can be set, pushing some metal over at each end and in the middle to hold the stone level. The rest of the metal can now be rubbed over the stone until it is smooth and flush against the stone. The brooch is now finished.

CUFF-LINKS

I use the spring-back form of cuff-link as explained earlier in Chapter 7, but the chain type can also be used. The back bar can either be oval or a scaled-down version of the top so that it will fit through the buttonhole.

On some 0.8mm sheet, mark out two diamonds 25mm long and 10mm wide. Mark on the vertical and horizontal centre lines. Cut the diamonds out and file the edges up.

Set the dividers to 1mm and mark right round the corners of the diamonds. Open up the dividers another 0.5mm and mark round again. From the vertical centre line,

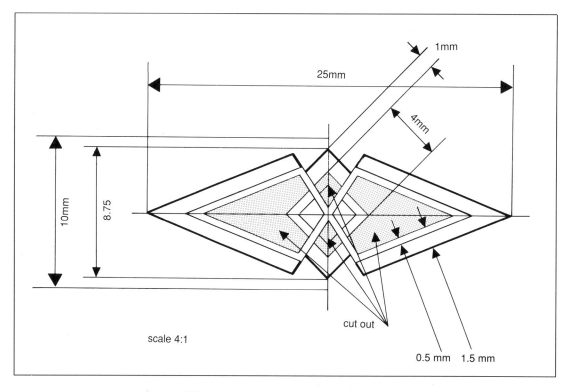

A plan view of the front of the cuff-link with the main dimensions.

use a ruler to mark off 1.5mm along the line just made that is 1mm in from the edge. Do the same on the line that is 0.5mm from the previous one. Repeat on the opposite side of the diamond.

Place the ruler on the mark made on the outside line in the top left quarter across to the mark on the inner line in the bottom right quarter and draw across. Move the ruler across so that it is positioned from the mark on the inside line in the top left quarter to the mark on the outer line in

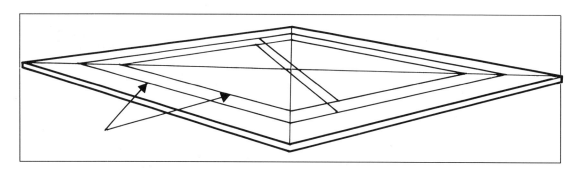

How to mark the top out where the wires go.

the bottom right quarter and draw across. Repeat this on the other side, in other words, from the top right quarter to the bottom left corner.

Draw down some square wire to 0.5mm in a different metal to the metal used for the diamond. If you are using silver and you want to have it hallmarked, you should use 9ct gold as your second metal. The marks that you made on the diamond are where the wire will be soldered on. The four longest lengths of wire are cut out first. File one end of the square wire flat and place the wire over the diamond where the longest length is marked. Mark this length off on the wire and then cut that length off. Place the wire over the diamond again and mark the angle that will form the point. File this angle on the wire, holding the length in a pin vice. Place the wire over the diamond again and mark the angle at the other end and file the end of the wire to an angle. Repeat this process for the other three long lengths.

The next four lengths to be cut and filed are for the cross in the centre. These are made in the same way as the longer lengths were made. Place the wire on one of the diagonals forming the cross in the centre. Mark the angle on the top where it will be soldered to the longer length already cut out. Mark across the wire at the centre and then cut the wire at this point. Repeat this process with the other three lengths of wire. File these lengths to the correct angle.

Two of the long lengths are then placed on the diamond to make sure that the angles are right. Make any necessary adjustments and then solder together to form a V shape. Next place two shorter

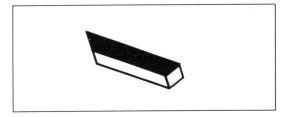

How the short length of wire will look.

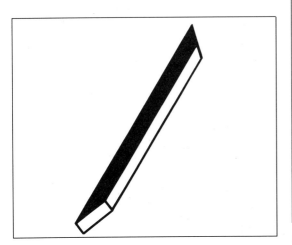

How the finished long length of wire will look.

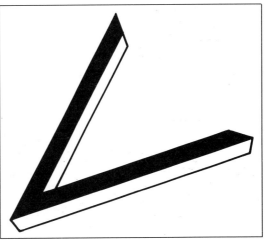

The two long lengths of wire that make up part of the wire pattern have been soldered together to form a V.

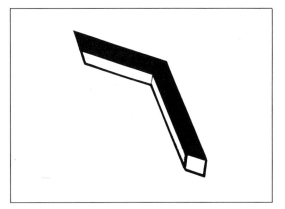

The two shorter lengths of wire have been soldered together to form a chevron shape.

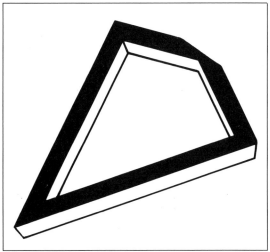

lengths on the diamond and check the angles. When they are correct, place them on a charcoal block and solder them together so that they form a chevron. Place the two longer lengths which form the V shape and the two shorter lengths which form the chevron together on the charcoal block to be soldered, so that they form a kite shape. Repeat this process with the other two lengths. On the ends formed by the two shorter lengths of wire, file away half the point, and then do the same on the other one. The two can then be soldered together to form the cross in the centre.

After cleaning in the pickle, the wire part of the design is filed flat on one side and soldered in place on the diamond.

With a ruler, draw a square in the centre of the cuff-link. The centres of the sides of the square pass through the ends of the cross in the centre of the cuff-link. With a centre punch, make a mark inside the narrow points formed by the wire design and drill a hole through this mark. Insert the saw blade through the hole and cut out the inside of the wire design leaving the point of the square in both sides.

One of the V shapes and one of the chevron shapes have been soldered together to form a kite shape. The point at the top of the kite shape has been filed half-way down to form a flat.

Two of the kite shapes have been soldered together at the points that have been filed flat.

130

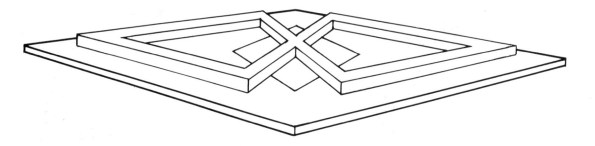

The square wire shape has been soldered in position on the diamond and a square marked out in the centre.

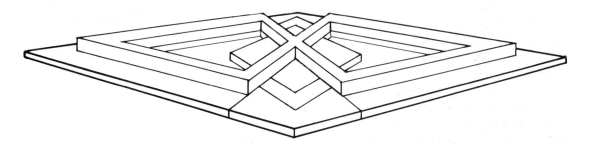

Two pieces are cut out from inside the wire design leaving two small squares against the centre. The Vs that are formed by the outside of the cross in the centre are extended out by drawing a line to the edge of the diamond. A mark 1mm out from the square has been made in the centre of the Vs to form a larger square.

The W shapes on either side of the centre have been cut out and also the squares in the V on either side, leaving a 1mm chevron shape between the Vs.

Cutting out between the wire designs on the cuff-link top.

Draw lines extending the V shapes formed on the outside of the wire design in the centre of the cuff-link. Mark off 1mm either side of the corner of the square inside the V shapes on both sides. Draw across at these marks so that the points of the square are enlarged. Cut out the corners of the square on the Vs then file them up. Cut out the W formed by these extended lines and the new larger point of the square, and file the edges.

The cuff-link spacer is made next. It is 11mm long and 6mm wide at one end; the other end is the width of the square in the centre of the cuff-link. Mark the spacer out on to some 0.8mm sheet. File a groove on the bottom of the 6mm end and file a 2mm flat in the centre. Solder a piece of 1.5mm square chenier, 2mm long, to the flat on the end, then solder the other end to the back of the cuff-link.

Emery the cuff-link front and the spacer through the grades. Give the two small squares inside the wire part of the

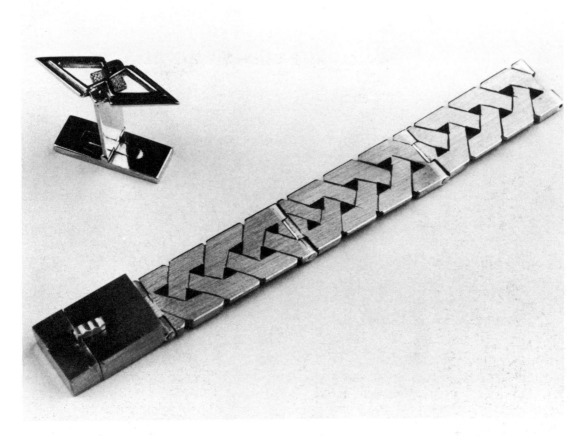

The finished cuff-link and a section of the finished bracelet.

design a hammered texture with the corner of the pointed end of a riveting hammer. Polish the rest of the cuff-link and spacer as well as the back, then rivet the back to the spacer by passing some wire through the round chenier on the back and the square chenier on the spacer. The cuff-link is now complete.

HINGED, PANELLED BRACELET

This project for a hinged, panelled bracelet uses a pierced design for the panels.

The total length of the bracelet is 184mm and it is made up of eight panels and the snap. The panels are each 20mm long and 10mm wide, and the snap is 15mm long. The rest of the length is made up by the hinges. The length of the bracelet can be altered by making the snap longer or by adding a small panel near the snap. This small panel can be 6mm, 13mm, or 16mm in length.

To make a hinge that is strong and hard wearing, use joint chenier drawn down to 2mm. The ends of the panels should also be made from 2mm sheet. As already stated in the section on hinges in Chapter 7, a

133

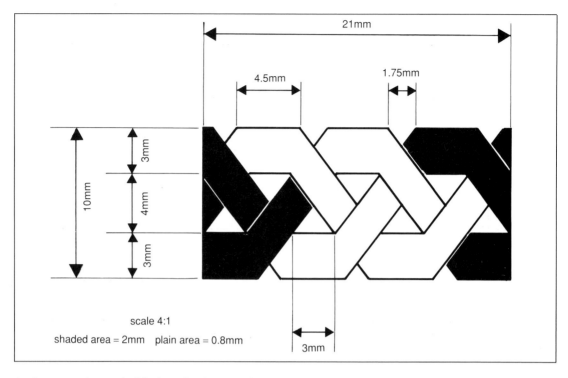

A plan view of a panel of the bracelet showing the main dimensions. The part not shaded on the panel can be made from a thinner metal.

stronger hinge is made if the area where the knuckles are to be soldered is the same thickness as the diameter of the knuckles. For this example I used a different coloured metal for the centre of the panels with 0.8mm sheet as it is easier to work. However, there is no reason why the whole panel cannot be made up in 2mm sheet of the same metal if you prefer. The area shaded on the plan is cut out from the thick 2mm sheet while the unshaded area is cut out from 0.8mm sheet. The snap is made from 0.5mm sheet.

Mark the pattern out on a sheet of paper – this is easy once the main measurements are known. Start by marking two parallel lines 10mm apart where the longest length can be marked out on the sheet. Once the basic pattern has been

marked on this strip, each part of the design can be marked fairly closely to one another.

Draw a vertical line at right angles through the two lines made. Make a mark 3mm in from the two parallel lines on either side, and draw across to give four parallel lines with two 3mm gaps and a 4mm gap. Starting on the inner of the two bottom lines, make a mark 3mm in from the vertical line and mark along the line in gaps of 3mm. Do the same for the line above. With a thicker pencil start on the line that was first marked out at 3mm intervals and mark in between every other mark, starting at the vertical line. Do the same for the line above, but draw the thick lines alternately to the ones just marked out below.

134

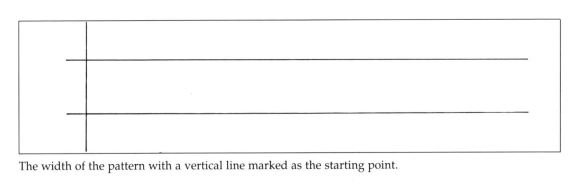

The width of the pattern with a vertical line marked as the starting point.

Two more horizontal lines are made inside the width of the bracelet 3mm in,
leaving 4mm between them.

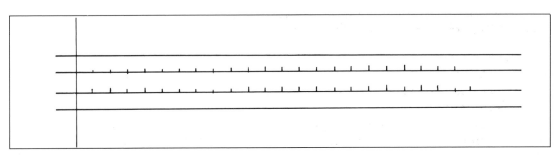

The two inner lines are marked off at 3mm intervals.

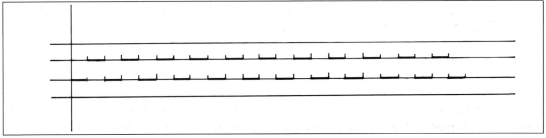

Every alternate 3mm space has been marked in with a heavier line. The top line
has been marked in the same way but alternately to the one below.

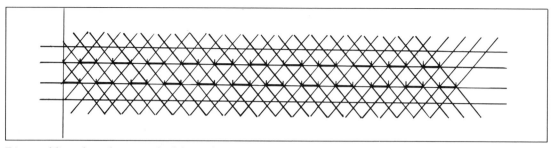

Diagonal lines have been marked from the end of one 3mm space on the bottom to the end of the 3mm space diagonally above it This is repeated in the opposite direction.

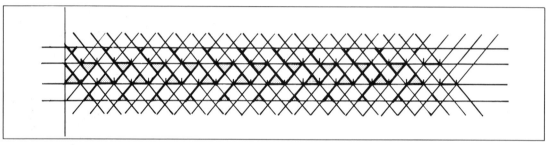

The pattern has been marked out in bold using this diagonal grid.

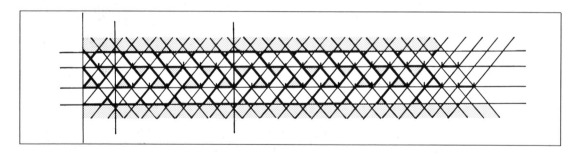

The sides of the pattern have been marked between the little Vs. The sections of panel can then be marked on.

Place one end of a ruler on the second line in from the bottom, against the vertical line. Place the other end against the first 3mm mark made on the line above and draw across continuing the line up through the top horizontal line. Keeping the ruler at the same angle, move it along to the next 3mm mark and draw another parallel line. Repeat until you reach the end of the marked out pattern. Repeat this process, but with the lines going in the opposite direction as shown in the diagram.

Next, mark the pattern out in a different

colour following the thicker lines on the diagram. Join up the small Vs on the top and bottom lines, leaving the V itself open. The pattern that forms the 2mm ends of each section can be shaded in on the paper so that the parts of the pattern that are shaded on the drawing are together at one end. The parts that are not shaded are together at the other end and will form the 0.8mm centre sections. The pieces can then be cut out and stuck on to the relevant pieces of metal using super-glue. If you use an ordinary glue it could lift as you are sawing.

When all twenty-four pieces making up the eight panels have been marked out, the metal can be cut out. Cut out the small triangles in the middle first. To do this, drill a hole and insert the piercing saw. These triangles are easier to cut out

The small triangles in the centre of the pattern are being cut out, before the pattern is cut out from the piece of sheet.

Filing the sides of the centre section flat.

as part of a larger sheet rather than a small section. When they have been cut out, file the pieces to the correct shape so that they are ready to be soldered together. On the thicker pieces of metal that form the ends of a panel, file a bevel on what will be the back below where it will be soldered to the thinner metal to form the centre.

For soldering, place the three parts of the panel upside-down on a charcoal block, so that the front is level. Borax the joints and heat up to boil off any excess water. Place a paillon of solder on the joint where the two parts meet. Heat the whole panel up and fully solder, allow to cool and place in the pickle. Repeat this process for the other seven panels. After

the panels have been dried, carefully file down the ends with a gapping file to form a groove half the depth of the chenier on all eight panels. The knuckles should then be cut to the right size. As the panel consists of three interweaving strips, three knuckles are used – the middle knuckle is 4mm long and the outer ones are 3mm long. File the ends of the chenier in a pin vice until they are flat. Make a slight bevel round the inside of the chenier hole with a drill, and then file a slight bevel round the edge. Pull the chenier out, mark its length, and then cut it generously outside the mark for the outside 3mm knuckles, but file it to the right length for the 4mm knuckles.

The three sections filed up to the right size are now ready to be soldered together.

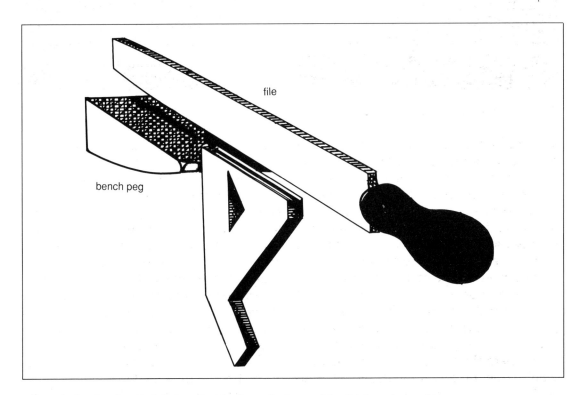

file

bench peg

A groove for the chenier is being filed in the end of one of the thicker pieces of metal.

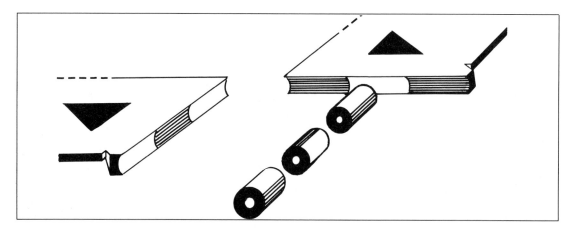

The ends of two of the panels. The shaded areas show the areas to be painted with the rouge mixture. The same is also shown on the knuckles.

Mark the length of the knuckles on the ends of the panels and then paint over the area where the knuckles will not be soldered with rouge. Place two panels upside-down on the charcoal block, and place the knuckles in their correct positions after the ends and half the sides have been painted with rouge. Place two lengths of steel wire through the centre to keep the knuckles in line. When the knuckles have been placed so that they are interlocking but not actually touching the other panel, they can be boraxed. After heating up to boil off the water, place a paillon of solder over the joint between the knuckle and the panel. They can then be soldered together fully.

The snap is a box snap and is made in the same way as the snap described in Chapter 7. Treat it in the same way as the panels when soldering on the knuckles, remembering to split the snap so that the two parts do not accidentally become soldered together. The panels should be placed the right way up for the knuckles to be soldered on as the snap is taller than the panel, unless you want the top of the snap flush with the top of the panels. Use easy solder for soldering the knuckles to the snap.

When the knuckles have all been soldered and cleaned in the pickle, file off any excess solder round them. When all the knuckles correctly fit into each other, file the ends flush with the sides of the panels, then file the tops and backs flat.

Clean up with emery all over and through all the grades. I have left a straight-grained finish as this gives a greater contrast between the two different metals than a polished finish would. If you have used only one type of metal, then a highly polished finish would be more desirable.

After polishing, the pattern is highlighted, as otherwise it could just look like a flat sheet of metal with some triangular holes in it. The pattern is marked back on with an engraver or a file – the former is preferable. First make sure that the engraver is very sharp – this is so that it leaves a well-defined cut and is less likely to slip as it is easier to push through the metal.

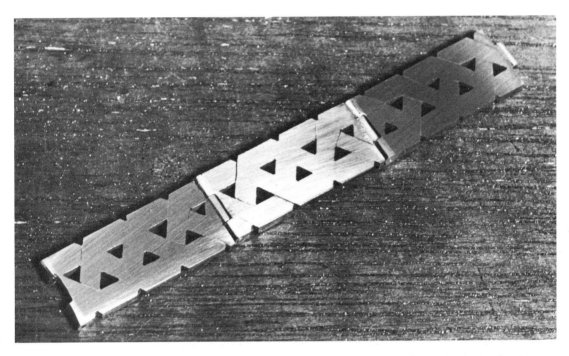

A section of the bracelet after the tops have been filed level and are ready to be straight-grained.

If you have straight-grained the tops, straight-grain them again to remove any burrs made by the engraving. If you have polished the tops, then the burrs will need to be removed with a burnisher. After the tops have been straight-grained, rub along the top corners with a burnisher to leave a polished edge running along the sides of the bracelet.

All that is left now is to rivet the panels together. Cut nine lengths of wire that are 1mm longer than the width of the bracelet. Clamp the wire in a pin vice and dome over the ends with a riveting hammer. When all nine are done, make a slight recess in the ends of the hinges on both sides. Place the wire through the hole in the hinge and then dome the other end. Go back and dome the first end until both ends are just proud of the hinge.

You should use a beading tool after riveting. This consists of a handle into which a series of different diameter lengths of rod can be placed. One end of the rod has a concave dish cut into it, and this will leave a round polished head when rubbed from side to side over the rivet.

INLAID RECTANGULAR BOX

Making a box gives you experience in forming accurate right-angled corners and soldering large items. By incorporating some inlay in the lid, you will see how simple one method of inlay can be. It will also give a professional finish to your box, especially as the bearers for the hinge will be made so that the lid will only open part way.

141

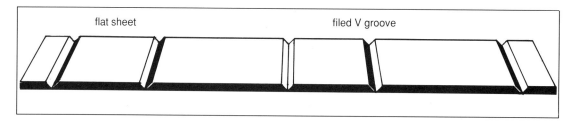

A strip of sheet (this will be the side of the box) has been filed across with a right-angled groove to form the corners. The grooves at either end will be filed through.

On some 1mm sheet from a square corner, mark a strip 20mm wide by 160mm long. Next use a square to mark across this strip the lengths of the sides, leaving a 5mm piece at either end. Cut out the strip and file the sides straight. With a triangular needle file, file up the five lines that will become the corners of the box. Check these lines with a square – they will need constant checking otherwise you will end up with an uneven box. After the lines have been opened out with the triangular needle file, use a square file to form a right-angled groove. File the strip all the way through at the two end lines. File the other three lines in the centre of the strip until a line underneath the groove can be seen on the back of the strip.

The strip can now be bent up to form a rectangular ring. Check each corner with the square, and alter as necessary, however, there is not much leeway for alteration. If the strip bends up to form a spiral, you have not filed the corners out square, and if this is not too drastic it can be remedied. However, there is a danger that the box will not sit flat. If the strip is out of line you will have to start again, remembering how much metal you have just wasted.

Bind round the rectangle to hold the two ends together and paint borax on the joints. After you have heated up the borax to boil off the water, place solder paillons evenly along the joints and a paillon of solder on the top. You can now solder and then place in the pickle to clean. File the top and bottom flat and the sides parallel, rubbing on flat emery finally to get the top and bottom completely flat.

Cut out two rectangles of sheet that are 1mm larger than the sides of the box. Rub over one of these rectangles with emery to clean it and place the box on top. Paint round with borax, heat up and place solder paillons evenly round the outside, then solder together.

Design the pattern for the inlay to go on the lid of the box. Trace the pattern on to some tracing paper and rub the back of the tracing paper with Plasticine. Place the tracing paper, Plasticine side down, on to the lid of the box where you want the design to be marked, and trace over the tracing paper with a pencil once again. Carefully lift off the tracing paper, and on the lid of the box there should be a faint outline left by the Plasticine. Draw over this outline with a scriber.

The next step is to cut out the design in the lid. Drill a hole through the areas that you want to cut out as near to an edge as possible. Pass the saw blade through the drill hole and cut the design out. Then file accurately up to the line.

Using the same method as before, mark

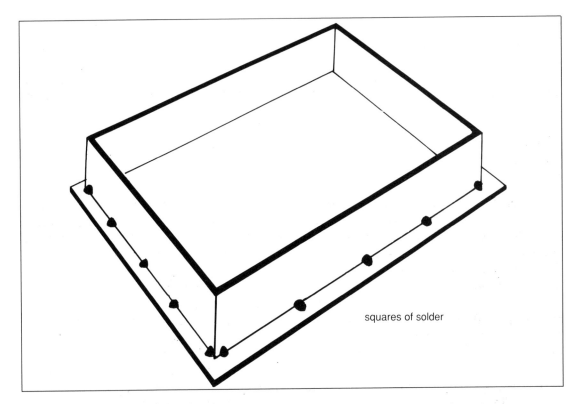

squares of solder

The rectangular ring is placed on some flat sheet that is slightly larger than the ring ready to be soldered. The placing of the paillons is shown.

out the design on the metal that is to be inlaid. Then cut this out slightly larger than required. File it up carefully so that it will fit exactly into the area in the lid that has been cut out.

When all the pieces of the design fit they can be soldered in place. The pieces are placed into their corresponding holes, borax is painted round the edge and this is then heated up to boil off the excess water. Place the paillons of solder round the edge of the piece that is to be soldered and heat the solder up so that it runs round the edge.

File up the side of the lid that will be on the inside, then mark round the depth of the lid on the rest of the box. Carefully cut through one corner on this line with a piercing saw – this will allow the air to escape from inside the box when the lid is soldered on. If a hole is not cut the box could explode as the air expands on heating when it is being soldered. Place the lid on the soldering block and then the rest of the box on top of it. Solder the two together.

The rest of the lid can now carefully be cut off with a piercing saw. File and emery the top and bottom flat where you have just cut through. On some 0.5mm sheet, mark out a strip 100mm long with one 50mm and two 25mm sides marked on it. Bend this up in the same way as the sides of the box, then solder it into the top of the box so that half its depth is left protruding. Make a mark 1.5mm down

143

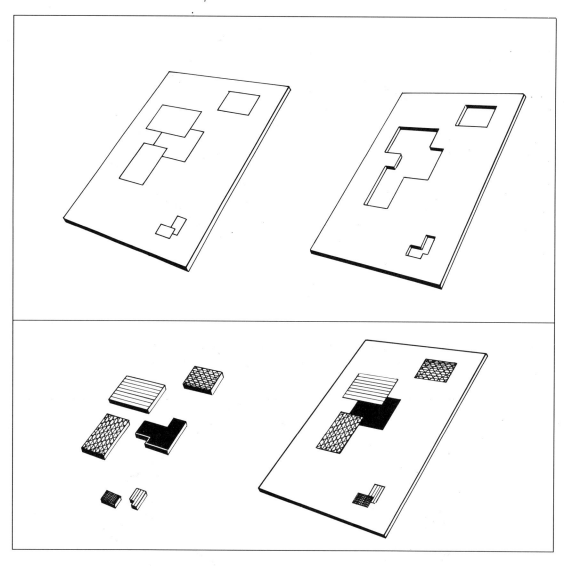

The inlay for the lid is done before the sheet that forms the top of the box is soldered in place. The stages of the inlaying process are shown. The shading denotes the different colours of the metals used.

across the back of the box with a pair of dividers. Cut this strip out and file flat, then do the same with the back of the lid.

Mark two strips on some 2mm thick sheet that are 50mm long and 5mm wide. After the strips have been cut out and filed to the correct size, mark the centre with some dividers and make a mark 1mm in from either edge. Make a mark 1mm in on each end of the same side, and another half-way along the short side to the centre line, and then cut this 1mm by 2mm piece out. This will enable the strip to fit into the back of the box.

144

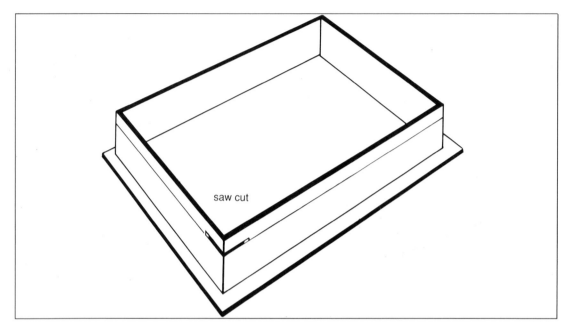

The depth of the lid has been marked round the top of the box. A saw cut has
been made through one corner on this line to allow air to exit the box as the top
is soldered on.

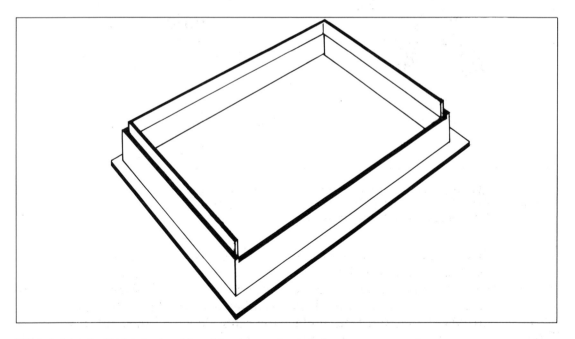

The bezel for the lid has been soldered in place and a strip has been cut out of
the back for the bearer to be seated in.

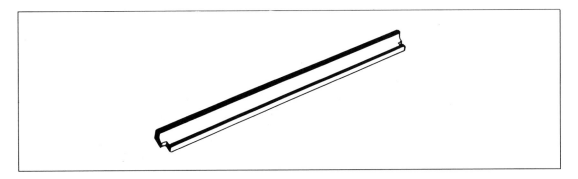

The bearer has had the groove filed in and two small notches made, so that the bearer length is the same as the inside of the box on one side, and the other side is the same length as the outside of the box.

With a 3mm gapping or parallel file, file carefully down the centre of the strips to a depth of 1.5mm. With a flat file, file the longer of the two sides down a short way and then at an angle down away from the groove on both strips. Place a strip upside-down on the soldering block and place the box in position over it and solder it in place. Do the same for the lid.

Cut two lengths of chenier to the exact length of the groove – 50mm. Mark the knuckles on to these two lengths of chenier – they should be 10mm long. File out two of the knuckles on one of the lengths, leaving a thin strip between the remain-

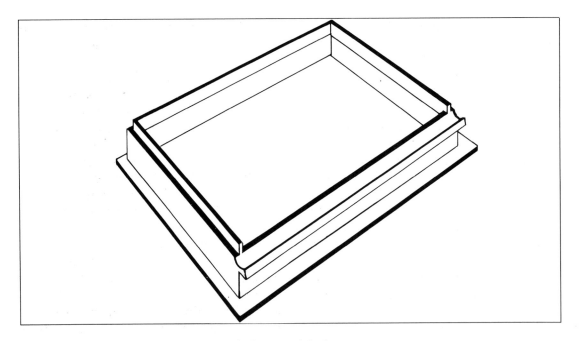

The bearer has been soldered in place on the bottom of the box.

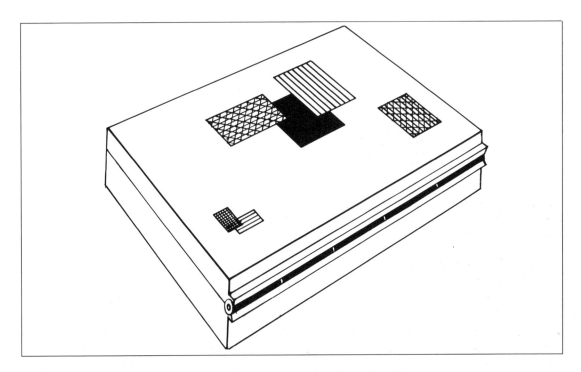

The finished box, seen from the back to show the bearers and knuckles. The inlay is also shown shaded on the lid.

ing three. Do the same for the other length of chenier, but only file the one in the middle out along with the two end ones.

Place the box on the soldering block after painting the area where there are no knuckles with rouge. Place the length of chenier with the three knuckles in the groove of the bearer and solder in place. Do the same for the lid after it has been painted with rouge, and solder the two knuckles in place. File out the strips that hold the knuckles the right distance apart. Fit the lid and the base of the box together and file to make any adjustments that are needed to the hinge. Broach out the hole through the centre of the hinge and taper some wire to fit in the hole.

Open the lid and see how far back it opens. It should open just past the verti-cal. If it does not open this far, file the two angles on the back of the bearers until it opens to your satisfaction.

File the top of the lid and the bottom of the box flush with the sides, and file the inlay on the top of the box flat now that all the soldering has been completed. The sides of the box may also need filing flat. Emery the box thoroughly, remembering to alternate the direction of emerying after each grade. The box can now be polished, taking care not to round the edges and corners.

The inside of the box can either be lined, or if the box is made from a precious metal, it can be plated. If the outside of the box is made from silver and has a lot of fire-stain on it, it can be plated as well as you might not want to spend time removing the fire-stain by hand.

Appendices

I FRACTIONAL, DECIMAL INCH, AND MILLIMETRE EQUIVALENTS

Fractions	Inches	mm	Fractions	Inches	mm	Fractions	Inches	mm	Fractions	Inches	mm
1/64	.0156	0.3969	9/64	.1406	3.5718	17/64	.2656	6.7468	25/64	.3906	9.9217
1/32	.0313	0.7937	5/32	.1562	3.9687	9/32	.2812	7.1437	13/32	.4062	10.3186
3/64	.0469	1.1906	11/64	.1719	4.3656	19/64	.2969	7.5405	27/64	.4219	10.7155
1/16	.0625	1.5875	3/16	.1875	4.7624	5/16	.3125	7.9374	7/16	.4375	11.1124
5/64	.0781	1.9843	13/64	.2031	5.1593	21/64	.3281	8.3343	29/64	.4531	11.5092
3/32	.0937	2.3812	7/32	.2187	5.5562	11/32	.3438	8.7312	15/32	.4687	11.9061
7/64	.1094	2.7781	15/64	.2344	5.9530	23/64	.3594	9.1280	31/64	.4844	12.3030
1/8	.1250	3.1750	1/4	.2500	6.3499	3/8	.3750	9.5249	1/2	.5000	12.6999

II TEMPERATURE CONVERSION TABLES

Fahrenheit to centigrade

°F	°C	°F	°C	°F	°C	°F	°C	°F	°C	°F	°C	°F	°C
32	0	660	349	960	516	1260	682	1560	849	1860	1015	2160	1182
212	100	680	360	980	527	1280	693	1580	860	1880	1026	2180	1193
400	204	700	371	1000	538	1300	704	1600	871	1900	1038	2200	1204
420	216	720	382	1020	549	1320	716	1620	882	1920	1049	2220	1216
440	227	740	393	1040	560	1340	727	1640	893	1940	1060	2240	1227
460	238	760	404	1060	571	1360	738	1660	904	1960	1071	2260	1238
480	249	780	416	1080	582	1380	749	1680	916	1980	1082	2280	1249
500	260	800	427	1100	593	1400	760	1700	927	2000	1093	2300	1260
520	271	820	438	1120	604	1420	771	1720	938	2020	1105	2320	1271
540	282	840	449	1140	616	1440	782	1740	949	2940	1116	2340	1284
560	293	860	460	1160	627	1460	793	1760	960	2060	1127	2360	1293
580	304	880	471	1180	638	1480	804	1780	971	2080	1138	2380	1305
600	316	900	482	1200	649	1500	816	1800	982	2100	1149	2400	1316
620	327	920	493	1220	660	1520	827	1820	993	2120	1160		
640	338	940	504	1240	671	1540	838	1840	1004	2140	1171		

Centigrade to Fahrenheit

°C	°F	°C	°F	°C	°F	°C	°F	°C	°F	°C	°F	°C	°F
0	32	330	626	480	896	630	1166	780	1436	930	1706	1080	1976
100	212	340	644	490	914	640	1184	790	1454	940	1724	1090	1994
200	392	350	662	500	932	650	1202	800	1472	950	1742	1100	2012
210	410	360	680	510	950	660	1220	810	1490	960	1760	1110	2030
220	428	370	698	520	968	670	1238	820	1508	970	1778	1120	2048
230	446	380	716	530	986	680	1256	830	1526	980	1796	1130	2066
240	464	390	734	540	1004	690	1274	840	1544	990	1814	1140	2084
250	482	400	752	550	1022	700	1292	850	1562	1000	1832	1150	2102
260	500	410	770	560	1040	710	1310	860	1580	1010	1850	1160	2120
270	518	420	788	570	1058	720	1328	870	1598	1020	1868	1170	2138
280	536	430	806	580	1076	730	1346	880	1616	1030	1886	1180	2156
290	545	440	824	590	1094	740	1364	890	1634	1040	1904	1190	2174
300	572	450	842	600	1112	750	1382	900	1652	1050	1922		
310	590	460	860	610	1130	760	1400	910	1670	1060	1940		
320	608	470	878	620	1148	770	1418	920	1688	1070	1958		

Comparison of thermometers
Freezing point = 32° Fahrenheit = 0° centigrade. Boiling point = 212° Fahrenheit = 100° centigrade
Cent × ⅑ + 32° = Fahr . Fahr − 32° × ⅚ = cent

III APPROXIMATE MELTING POINTS OF METALS

Platinum	1,755°C
Fine gold	1,063°C
22ct gold	1,003°C
18ct gold	905°C
14ct gold	840°C
9ct gold	830°C
Fine silver	961°C
Britannia silver	920°C
Standard or sterling silver	890°C
Titanium	1,675°C
Copper	1,083°C
Brass	940°C
Nickel	1,455°C
Aluminium	660°C
Tin	232°C
Zinc	420.4°C
Iron	1,539°C
Lead	327.4°C
Steel	1,350°C

IV APPROXIMATE ANNEALING TEMPERATURES FOR METALS

Platinum	950°C
Fine gold	Annealing not required
18ct gold	650°C
14ct gold	650°C
9ct gold	650°C
Fine silver	Annealing not required
Sterling silver	625°C
Aluminium	325°C
Nickel	665°C
Copper	650°C
Brass	625°C

V APPROXIMATE MELTING POINTS OF SOLDERS

Silver Solders

Hard	745–775°C
Medium	720–765°C
Easy	705–725°C
Extra easy	667–705°C

Gold Solders (Yellow)

18ct hard	815–825°C
18ct medium	740–750°C
18ct easy	630–705°C
9ct hard	755–792°C
9ct medium	720–760°C
9ct easy	695–715°C
9ct extra easy	640–650°C

VI APPROXIMATE SPECIFIC GRAVITY OF METALS

Platinum	21.4
Fine gold	19.5
18ct gold	15.6
14ct gold	13.4
9ct gold	11.3
Fine silver	10.5
Sterling silver	10.4
Titanium	4.5
Aluminium	2.7
Copper	8.9
Brass	8.5

Note: This is a useful table if you wish to calculate the cost of copying a piece of work using a different metal. To calculate the cost, take the weight of the original and multiply by the specific gravity of the copy, then divide this by the specific gravity of the original. Multiply the answer by the cost per gram of the metal you wish to use.

151

VII ADDITIONAL HALLMARKS

Former Assay Office Marks

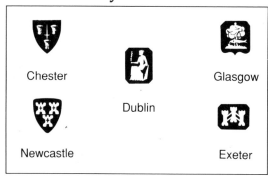

Chester

Dublin

Glasgow

Newcastle

Exeter

Duty Marks

George III

Victoria

Commemorative Marks

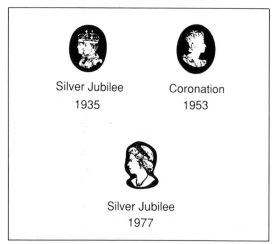

Silver Jubilee
1935

Coronation
1953

Silver Jubilee
1977

VIII   LONDON SILVER HALLMARKS

Year	Letter	Year	Letter	Year	Letter	Year	Letter	Year	Letter	Year	Letter	Year	Letter
1678	a	1712		1744	i	1780	e	1815	U	1850	P	1888	N	1958	C
1679	b	1713		1745	k	1781	f	1816	a	1851	Q	1889	O	1959	d
1680	c	1714		1746	l	1782	g	1817	b	1852	R	1890	P	1923	h	1960	e
1681	d	1715		1747	m	1783	h	1818	C	1853	S	1891	Q	1924	i	1961	f
1682	e	1716	A	1748	n	1784	i	1819	d	1854	T	1892	R	1925	k	1962	g
1683	f	1717	B	1749	O	1785	k	1820	e	1855	U	1893	S	1926	l	1963	h
1684	g	1718	C	1750	P	1786	l	1821	f	1856	a	1894	T	1927	m	1964	i
1685	h	1719	D	1751	q	1787	m	1822	g	1857	b	1895	U	1928	n	1965	k
1686	i	1720	E	1752	r	1788	n	1823	h	1858	c	1896	a	1929	o	1966	l
1687	k	1721	F	1753	t	1789	o	1824	i	1859	d	1897	b	1930	p	1967	m
1688	l	1722	G	1754	t	1790	p	1825	k	1860	e	1898	c	1931	q	1968	n
1689	m	1723	H	1755	u	1791	q	1826	l	1861	f	1899	d	1932	r	1969	o
1690	n	1724	I	1756	A	1792	r	1827	m	1862	g	1900	e	1933	s	1970	P
1691	o	1725	K	1757	B	1793	s	1828	n	1863	h	1901	f	1934	t	1971	q
1692	p	1726	L	1758	C	1794	t	1829	o	1864	i	1902	g	1935	u	1972	r
1693	q	1727	M	1759	D	1795	u	1830	p	1865	k	1903	h	1936	A	1973	s
1694	r	1728	N	1760	E	1796	A	1831	q	1866	l	1904	i	1937	B	1974	t
1695	s	1729	O	1761	F	1797	B	1832	r	1867	m	1905	k	1938	C		
1696	t	1730	P	1762	G	1798	C	1833	s	1868	n	1906	l	1939	D	1975	A
1697	a	1731	Q	1763	H	1799	D	1834	t	1869	o	1907	m	1940	E	1976	B
1698		1732	R	1764	I	1800	E	1835	u	1870	p	1908	n	1941	F	1977	C
1699		1733	S	1765	K	1801	F	1836	A	1871	q	1909	o	1942	G	1978	D
1700		1734	T	1766	L	1802	G	1837	B	1872	r	1910	p	1943	H	1979	E
1701	ff	1735	V	1767	m	1803	H	1838	C	1873	s	1911	q	1944	I	1980	F
1702		1736	a	1768	N	1804	I	1839	D	1874	t	1912	r	1945	K	1981	G
1703		1737	b	1769	O	1805	K	1840	E	1875	u	1913	s	1946	L	1982	H
1704		1738	C	1770	P	1806	L	1841	F	1876	A	1914	t	1947	M	1983	I
1705		1739	d	1771	Q	1807	M	1842	G	1877	B	1915	u	1948	N	1984	K
1706		1739		1772	R	1808	N	1843	H	1878	C	1916	a	1949	O	1985	L
1707		1740	e	1773	S	1809	O	1844	I	1879	D	1917	b	1950	P	1986	M
1708		1741	f	1774	T	1810	P	1845	K	1880	E	1918	c	1951	Q	1987	N
1709		1742	g	1775	U	1811	Q	1846	L	1881	F	1919	d	1952	R	1988	O
1710		1743	h	1776	a	1812	R	1847	M	1882	G	1920	e	1953	S		
1711				1777	b	1813	S	1848	N	1883	H	1921	f	1954	T		
				1778	C	1814	T	1849	O	1884	I	1922	g	1955	U		
				1779	d					1885	K			1956	a		
										1886	L			1957	b		
										1887	M						

153

Glossary

Alloy   A mixture of two or more metals.

Annealing   A process used to heat and then cool metal to bring it to a fully soft and unstressed condition.

Anodizing   A process which uses an electrical current to colour metal.

Argo-tech   A chemical that inhibits fire-stain.

Bearer   A thickness of metal which the hinge knuckles are soldered to, or which is used to strengthen an area where a hinge is to go.

Bevel   A flat area filed on the edge of a piece of metal.

Bezel   A flange that holds a gem in place.

Binding wire   Steel wire that is very flexible and is used to bind pieces of metal together when soldering.

Broachers   A five-sided, tapered length of steel used for enlarging holes.

Burnisher   A tool made of polished steel which is used to push metal over stones.

Burr   1.   A tool that fits in a pendant motor for enlarging or tapering holes.
2.   A thin strip of metal left round the edges after sawing, filing or drilling.

Carat   Unit of measure which indicates the content of gold in an alloy.

Chasing   A method of applying surface decoration to metal from above using a variety of punches and hammers.

Cheniers   The name given in jewellery making to tubes.

Collet   1.   A device for holding a cylindrical work piece within the taper of a machine-tool spindle.

2.   A name given to a conical stone setting.

Draw plate   An instrument used for reducing the gauge of wires and for shaping them.

Emery   Abrasive material used in the finishing process of metal.

Fire-stain   The mark made by copper coming to the surface on sterling silver after heating to a high temperature.

Flux   A chemical in liquid or paste form used to aid the flow of solder and to impede oxide formation on metal surfaces.

Jump ring   Small rings made of wire that are used to hold findings to main components.

Knuckles   Short lengths of chenier that form a hinge.

Laps   These are used to hold polishing compounds while polishing.

Mops   Round discs of cloth used for polishing.

Oxidizing   A method of blackening areas of metal to accent a design.

Pickle   An acid solution to clean the fire-scale and flux residue that remains on metal after heating or soldering.

Planishing   A process for smoothing metals by hammering with polished hammers over metal stakes.

Repoussé   A method of surface decoration as in chasing, only the decoration is beaten up from the underside.

Reticulation   A method of creating textural surface on metal by building up a fire-skin and melting the metal between the surfaces.

Rifflers   Shaped files used for filing awkward corners.

Rolling   Reducing of a gauge of metal by running it through a rolling mill under pressure.

Solder   An alloy of metals that can be melted to form a joint between metal components.

Stop-out   The liquid that is painted on metal to resist the acid used in etching.

Swarf   The metal shavings formed by machining operations.

Vernier gauge   An instrument that will measure the inside, outside and depth of components.

Work-hardened   A state caused by filing, sawing, hammering or bending the metal, which compresses the molecules of the metal causing it to become hard.

Useful Addresses

ASSAY OFFICES

Goldsmiths' Hall,
Gutter Lane,
London EC2V BAQ.

Newhall Street,
Birmingham B3 1SB.

137 Portobello Street,
Sheffield S1 4DR.

15 Queen Street,
Edinburgh EH2 1JE.

INFORMATION

British Crafts Council,
43 Earlham Street,
London WC2H 9LD.

Crafts Council,
8 Waterloo Place,
London SW1Y 4AU.

The Worshipful Company of Goldsmiths,
Goldsmiths' Hall,
Foster Lane,
London EC2V 6BN.

TOOLS

Frank Pike,
Hatton Wall,
London EC1.
(Tel: 071 405 2688)

Le Ronker,
84 Vyse Street,
Hockley,
Birmingham B18 6HA.
(Tel: 021 507 0267)

A. Shoot & Sons,
116–118 St John's Street,
London EC1.
(Tel: 071 253 9462/4)

Thomas Sutton Ltd.,
37 Frederick Street,
Birmingham B1 3HN.

H. S. Walsh & Sons Ltd.,
12–16 Clerkenwell Road,
London EC1N 8JJ.
(Tel: 071 405 5928)

H. S. Walsh & Sons Ltd.,
1–2 Warstone Mews,
Wartstone Lane,
Birmingham B18 6JB.
(Tel: 021 236 9346)

BULLION DEALERS

J. Blunell & Sons, Ltd.,
199 Wardour Street,
London W1V 4JN.
(Tel: 071 437 4746)

Johnson Matthey Metals Ltd.,
43 Hatton Garden,
London EC1N 8EE.
(Tel: 071 269 8103)

Johnson Matthey Metals Ltd.,
Vittoria Street,
Birmingham B1 3NZ.
(Tel: 021 200 2120)

Metalor Ltd.,
74 Warstone Lane,
Birmingham B18 6NG.
(Tel: 021 236 3568)

TOOLS, FINDINGS AND A LIMITED SUPPLY OF BULLION

Exchange Findings Ltd.,
11–13 Hatton Wall,
London EC1N 8HX.
(Tel: 071 831 7574)

PLATERS AND GILDERS

Eric Parker,
49 Britten Street,
London EC1M 5NA.
(Tel: 071 250 0700)

W. Pairpoint & Sons Ltd.,
10 Shacklewell Road,
London N16 7TA.
(Tel: 071 254 6362)

STONE SUPPLIERS

Chas Mathews & Sons Ltd.,
7 Hatton Garden,
London EC1.
(Tel: 071 405 7333)

Keith Mitchell,
Hatton House,
20 Holborn,
London EC1.
(Tel: 071 242 3404)

Index

Italic numerals denote page numbers of illustrations.

Alum   48
Annealing   16, 46–8
Arkansas stone   51
Argo-tect   45

Barrel snap   79, 80–1
Beading tool   141
Binding wire   46, 59
Bolt ring   67
Borax dish   28
Box snap   79, 82–90
Box to make   141–7
Bracelet to make   *114*, 133–41
Broacher   30
  in use   102
Brooch pins   72–8
  to make   *114*, 121–7
Buff sticks   49, 56
Burnisher   27, *28*
  to use   103–4

Carat paper   50
Carborundum   51
Centre punch   27, *28*
Charcoal block   33, 46
Chasing   112–13
Cheniers   77–8, 91
Collets   27, 106–7, 115–17
Cufflinks   *114*, 127–33
  backs   67, 97–101

Designing   14, 114–15
Diamondtine   54
Dies   34–5
Dividers   27, *28*, 59
Doming block and punches   34
Draw plates   32–3
Draw tongs   32–3
Drills, bow   30
  hand   29, *31*
  pillar   18
  spade   102

twist   29–30

Ear-ring findings   67, 68–71
Emery paper   49–50
Enamelling   113
Engraving   112
Etching   111–12
Eyeglass   33

Files   21–5
  hand and needle   21–2
  barrette or safety back   23–4
  crossing or oval   23
  escapement   25
  flat   22
    in use   63–4
  half-round   22
  round or rat tail   23
  square   23
  three-square or triangular   22–3
  others
    gapping   24, 91
      in use   92
    parallel   24, 91
      in use   92
    riffler   22, 25
    slotting   25
Findings   67–109
Fire-resistant block   46
Fire stain   36
Flux   44–5
Fraizers   18

Gravers   32

Hallmarking   38–40, 116
Hammered textures   111
Hammers, planishing   28–9, 111
  riveting   28, *30*
  small ball pein   28, *30*
    in use   111
Hinges   91–7

Inlay   111

Jump rings   67–8

Knuckles   93–6

Metals   36–40
  ferrous
    steel   24, 38
  non ferrous
    aluminium   36, 38
    brass   24, 37
    copper   36, 37, 38
    gilding   37
    lead   36
    monel   38
    nickel   38
    tin   38
    titanium   38
    zinc   37, 38
  precious
    gold   36–7
    platinum   36, 37
    silver   36, 37
Micrometer   31
Mouth-blown torch   29, 42

Natural stone   50–1

Oil stone dust   54

Paillons   27, 29, 44
Pendant motor   13, 17–18
Pickle   48
Piercing saw   19–21
Pliers   25–27
  flat-nose   25, 26, 27
  half round   25, 26, 27
  parallel   25, 26
  round-nose   25, 26
Pin vice   30, 31
Polishing   49–57
Polishing compounds   53–4
Polishing cone   66
Polishing mops   17, 53–6
Polishing motor   15, 17, 52–3, 54–5
Punches   34, 35, 111

Rawhide mallet   28, 30
Repoussé   112

Reticulation   110
Ring, to make
  claw setting   115–17
  rubbed-over setting   114, 117–21
  simple   58–66
Ring mandrel   32
  in use   59
Ring sizes   32
  in use   59
Ring stick   32
  in use   59
Riveting   102
Rolled textures   111
Rolling mill   16–17
Ruler   27, 28

Safety   14–15
Safety chains   67
Scratch brush   110
Saw blades   19–21
Scorpers   32
Screw plate   34–5
Scriber   27, 28
Shears   27, 29
Side cutter   28
Solder   29, 43–4
  to solder   41–7, 61–2
Soldering blocks   33, 46
  torches   28, 29, 41–3
Spreading tool   102
Square   27, 28
Stone setting
  crown   104–7
  claw   107–9
  rub over 102–4
Stopout   111–12
Swage block   33

Taps   34–5
Triblet   32
Tweezers   28, 48

Veniers   31
Vices   11

Workbench   12–13
Workshop   11–17
Water of ayr stone   36, 50–1
Wet and dry paper   50

Other titles in the Crowood Manual of Techniques series:

Bookbinding   Pamela Richmond
Furniture Making   Anthony Hontoir
Metalworking   Mike George
Pottery   Doug Wensley
Relief Print-Making Colin Walklin
Weaving   Rosemary Bridgman
Woodcarving   Reg Parsons
Woodturning   Hugh O'Neill